100 Years of Teamsters History

A STRONG LEGACY
A POWERFUL FUTURE

100 YEARS
INTERNATIONAL BROTHERHOOD OF TEAMSTERS
1903-2003

INTERNATIONAL
BROTHERHOOD OF TEAMSTERS

First published in the United States by DeLancey Publishing, Inc. 2003

Printed and bound in the U.S.A. by DeLancey Printing, Inc.

Contents

INTERNATIONAL
BROTHERHOOD OF TEAMSTERS
AFL-CIO

OFFICE OF
JAMES P. HOFFA
GENERAL PRESIDENT

C. THOMAS KEEGEL
GENERAL SECRETARY-TREASURER

Dear Reader,

A cardinal rule for the labor movement—and for life in general—is that one must study the past in order to better prepare for the future. That is why we take great pleasure in presenting this inspiring review of the first century in the life of the International Brotherhood of Teamsters.

For 100 years, the Teamsters Union has been at the forefront in the struggle for worker rights in North America. As our vast continent became linked by the world's most comprehensive network of highways, the transportation industry experienced explosive growth—as did the need for strong union representation.

The earliest Teamsters were drivers and stablemen. By building on the strength of those workers, today's Teamsters Union is more diverse than ever—encompassing workers in every imaginable occupation. Yet while our professions have evolved, our union maintains its commitment to guaranteeing a safe and fair workplace, a secure retirement and a decent standard of living for every Teamster and their family.

The Teamsters story is the story of the North American worker—a story of struggle and sacrifice, heartbreaking setbacks and enormous accomplishments. As you browse through the pages of this book, we invite you to share in the celebration of our union's heritage—and to join us as we learn from our proud legacy and build a powerful future.

Fraternally,

James P. Hoffa
General President

C. Thomas Keegel
General Secretary-Treasurer

Preface

Over the past 100 years, the Teamsters Union has helped millions of workers achieve the American Dream. From the turn of the century when disconnected locals of team drivers began to unify under the same banner until today when 1.4 million Teamsters work in every imaginable profession, the Teamsters has been instrumental in creating the middle class. Our success is a testament to collective bargaining. Without unions, working men and women would have no weekends, no pensions and no health insurance. Looking back over this Teamster Century we see that from every contract, every strike, every successful grievance and organizing victory, we have built a foundation. And it is from this foundation that we build our future.

The growth of the Teamsters cannot be measured in neatly dated segments, nor achievements attributed solely to particular administrations or eras. Success is often best measured over time, as improvements in standards of living and the workplace become evident. The best way to celebrate the Teamster Century is to highlight the actions and events that brought those improvements to working families and their communities.

In setting out to commemorate those past efforts and achievements, it became apparent that the heart of the story came from the everyday struggles, triumphs and dreams of rank-and-file members. It has always been the working men and women who proudly displayed their union cards that make up the character of the Teamsters. They walked picket lines in the rain and snow, took the time to show young members the right way to do a job and encouraged others seeking to organize and join the union. The content of a union's character is the factor that determines whether it will survive or fade away over time. The Teamsters survived. This is the story of those who made it happen.

Opposite:
Teamsters Headquarters
141 E. Market Street,
Indianapolis, Indiana.
1903-1909

To fully appreciate the Teamsters as an organization—and to set goals for the future of the union—great traditions must be recognized. Teamster members must understand the struggles of the past century to build a better future for the generations to come.

Organizers, leaders and active members must be familiar with significant events in the union's past. Every Teamster will feel more committed to the workings of the present day—and have a more rewarding experience as a member—if they understand the union's proud tradition and heritage. The old photographs and mementos in this book are not half-forgotten events that were over and done with long ago. They represent the foun-

dation of a bridge that will carry us into the future.

The founding members of the union foresaw the growth and promise of the Teamsters as a model for workers everywhere. And they developed a philosophy that is as true and vital today as it was in 1903. That philosophy states:

"Let each member do his duty as he sees fit. Let each put his shoulder to the wheel and work together to bring about better results. Let no member sow seeds of discord within our ranks, and let our enemies see that the Teamsters of this country are determined to get their just rewards and to make their organization as it should be—one of the largest and strongest trade unions in the country now and beyond."

Proud Teamsters
Delegates at the 1907 Teamsters Convention.

Coming Together:

The Early Years

From the early days of our nation, the men who drove horse-drawn wagons played an essential role in American commerce. Trade and delivery of goods would have come to a virtual standstill without the hard work and risks undertaken by these team drivers or "teamsters" as they were known. Despite the importance and necessity of their work, life was not easy for them. Jobs were not secure and often scarce in low seasons or difficult economic periods in the country. When a job was available, the workload was heavy and frequently dangerous as decent transportation routes were nonexistent. The men labored 12 to 18 hours per day, seven days a week for an average wage of $2.00 per day with the cost of any lost or damaged goods deducted from their wages.

By the end of the 19th Century, teamsters were fed up with poor treatment and began to join together to improve their working conditions. In 1898, team drivers in the Midwest organized into 18 local unions.

This activity caught the attention of Samuel Gompers, President of the American Federation of Labor (AFL). He began urging the locals to form a national union and join the AFL. Local unions agreed and in 1899, the Team Drivers International Union (TDIU) was formed with a membership of 1,700.

By 1902, the union had grown to 13,800 members, but there was trouble brewing. Several locals in the Chicago area were unhappy with an increase in the per capita tax paid by the locals to the International Union and they strongly disagreed with the TDIU's policy of allowing drivers who owned up to five teams to join the union. The Chicago members

Feeding the Horse
This Teamster is feeding his horse during the rush of a busy day. Early Teamsters bargained for a noontime feeding of their horses. The horse team had to be kept in good shape so the Teamster could earn a paycheck.
c. 1910

Opposite:
Newspaper Delivery
Newspaper delivery workers navigating the streets of New York City faced many challenges.
c. 1900

The Early Teamster
A Teamster from Green Transfer Company in Portland, Oregon stands proudly in front of his horse and carriage.
1908

eventually split from the TDIU and formed their own union—the Teamsters National Union. There were now two unions representing teamsters, one affiliated with the AFL and one independent union.

A New Union is Formed

In spite of the formal break, most rank-and-file members quickly realized that two unions were an unnecessary drain on time, energy and resources, and began to debate possible alternatives. Gompers once again helped foster a solution that led to a unified national membership. After much discussion with the two separate unions about their interests and concerns, Gompers helped organize an amalgamation convention held in August of 1903 in Niagara Falls, New York.

Delegates were sent from each of the two groups to work out their differences. Although not all disagreements and rivalries were settled, a new union for the teaming craft—the International Brotherhood of Teamsters—emerged. The new union soon became recognized as a powerful force in American labor.

The first Teamsters were proud of their craft and the lead-

George Innis *(far left) was President of the Team Drivers International Union. He continued in a leadership role with the formation of the International Brotherhood of Teamsters.* Albert Young *(left) was President of the Teamsters National Union. c. 1903*

ing role they played as part of the backbone of American industry. But they also understood that changing the perception of the "working man" held by business and industry leaders as well as the "polite" middle classes, was no easy task.

Improving wages and working conditions would take enormous effort. Despite the Teamsters ever-increasing numbers and strong desire for dignity and justice on the job, members still struggled with obstacles placed before them by business and government. There were few laws protecting workers, and companies used anti-trust laws—which were originally aimed at controlling company monopolies—to halt the progress of the rising labor movement.

In 1905, the Teamsters went on strike at the Montgomery Ward Company in Chicago. The strike lasted 100 days and became very violent, resulting in 21 deaths and an estimated $1 million in fiscal loss to the union. In the end, the company's cutthroat tactics broke the strike. This defeat led to a change in leadership. At the 1907 convention a new president

Daniel J. Tobin *served as General President of the Teamsters for 45 years.*

Sympathy Strikers *in 1905 join with 4,600 Chicago Teamsters against Montgomery Ward. The strike was broken, and the rising discontent helped pave the way for Dan Tobin to win the General Presidency in 1907.*

13

Milk Delivery
*An early Teamster delivers
milk to restaurants.
c. 1907*

was chosen, one with strong national support and new ideas
for the future. The election of Dan Tobin as General President
of the Teamsters brought renewed momentum to the organization, and started the fledgling group on a path that would
change the face of the labor movement.

Expanding The Membership

The Teamsters now entered into a period of aggressive organizing which resulted in a broadening of the membership base
as well as increased revenue and recognition. Workers in areas
not traditionally associated with team drivers, such as gravel
haulers, beer wagon drivers, and deliverymen for bakeries,

**Wagon Maker and
Blacksmith Shop**
*that evolved into
Fruehauf Trailer Co.
c. 1900*

Log Rolling
Workers move tree trunks down a trail in the Oregon mountains. c. 1910

joined the union. By 1909, new crafts led to a name change that more accurately described the growing membership. The union became known as International Brotherhood of Teamsters, Chauffeurs, Stablemen and Helpers.

As the Teamsters grew in stature and became more confident in its ability to protect members in the workplace, the success rate of its efforts increased. The union was winning strikes, contracts were becoming standardized and benefits were won that reduced hours and increased pay.

The Teamsters were also becoming known as leaders on issues of social justice. In 1912, the union set a precedent when delegates to the convention voted not to accept or allow any entertainment by non-union employees. Further, the union was one of the very first to recognize the importance of organizing women. As early as 1917, Teamsters were representing women employed in the laundry industry, with the group even being advised and supported at bargaining talks by women representatives. Some locals instituted "open meetings" inviting members' wives, mothers and friends to attend with the goal of getting more women involved in the labor movement.

Delivering Beer
In the days before motorized lift gates and pallet jacks, it took two Teamsters to move beer barrels off of the beer wagon. c. 1905

Women in the Workforce

The number of women entering the workforce increased greatly with the onset of World War I. They took on many jobs traditionally held by men, such as maintaining vehicles and machinery. c. 1920

Instrument for Change

Teamsters also demonstrated openness to racial equality, being able to boast, "Teamsters know no color line." Part of the contract for female laundry workers in 1917 included a non-negotiable provision that black women must be paid equally to white women. By World War I, the Teamsters were on their way to being one of the most diverse organizations in the country.

And on a number of occasions Teamsters took direct action on behalf of their horses, demanding better food and care for them when the bosses insisted on speed-ups in the

highly competitive industries. The Teamsters won each time.

The industrial revolution hit the Teamsters as it did all of the skilled trades and crafts. In 1910, technological progress began to affect the Teamsters at their very heart. Horses—their faithful partners—were being outmoded with the advent of the motorized truck. It would be years before horses were completely retired, but the union was quick to see that the motor truck was the way of the future and acted accordingly.

Efforts were made to organize workers in newly forming motor truck companies. And the Teamsters sought to include truck drivers in contracts with companies that utilized both horses and motorized vehicles. In 1912, Teamsters were involved in the first transcontinental delivery of goods by motor truck. As a result of that event and other similar experiences, the union became a staunch advocate for improved roads and driver safety training.

Legislation passed in the years just prior to World War I eased some of the struggles on union members. The Clayton Anti-Trust Act declared that unions were not unlawful under the Sherman Anti-Trust provisions, and workers compensation bills were passed in most states. Union contracts also resulted in shorter days, giving workers some "leisure hours" often for the first time in their lives.

Adapting to Change
William Lee, a driver for the Ward Baking Co. with his horse and wagon in 1916 and again in 1917 with the first motor truck the company owned. Lee later served as President of Local 734.

Tobacco Motor Truck
*Delivery times were
shortened with the advent
of the motorized truck.
c. 1918*

Transitions on the Road
*Varied toll rates reflect the
growing changes in
transportation. c. 1912*

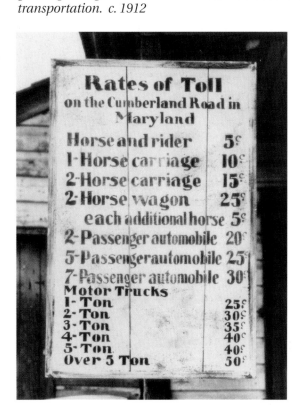

Hope for the Future

As the country entered into World War I, the Teamsters had developed a fair amount of political and economic leverage. Union officers, particularly General President Tobin, were recognized as national leaders and were asked to serve on various government advisory committees and international labor conferences. Many rank-and-file members served on service and reform committees in their local areas. The government realized that to establish and sustain the war effort, the full cooperation of the Teamsters would be needed. Union members collected and delivered supplies, attended rallies, purchased war bonds and helped in relief efforts for families of soldiers and war victims overseas.

As union men went abroad as combat soldiers or support personnel, women stepped up to take over the jobs that they left behind. More women than ever entered the workforce and the union was concerned that unscrupulous employers would view these workers as easy targets.

Organizing efforts were increased and Teamster women were given additional training in bargaining tactics and other skills to keep the union running smoothly during the war. Teamsters adopted the national slogan, "Equal pay for equal work," leaving no question that it was strongly supportive of its female members.

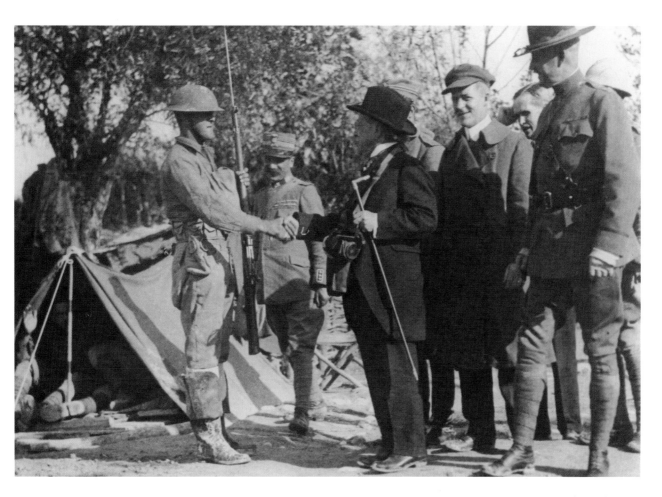

The war brought about unavoidable social changes. New inventions and technologies included both marvels and horrors, and seemed to emphasize and quicken the pace of the world's move into the "modern age." The Teamsters were determined not to be left behind.

The years following World War I held many ups and downs for the union. Economic forces, increased immigrant labor, changing perceptions of the labor movement and growing differences in practices, values and ideology in the labor movement itself would all play a role in the future of the Teamsters. But for a group that in less than two decades had gone from a fledgling union with only a few thousand members to a powerful voice for the working class, wearing the union pin was not just a habit or requirement but a source of true pride and hope for the future.

Teamsters in World War I
Teamsters were involved in all aspects of war service both at home and abroad.

Top: Samuel Gompers pays the doughboys a visit. 1918

Above: Teamsters had an advantage over their fellow soldiers as they were already familiar with "motor trucks." c. 1917

AMERICAN

FEDERATION OF LABOR

— DOTH GRANT THIS —

Certificate of Affiliation

To   Ed. Gould   M. Dwyer

J. B. Fitzpatrick   H. H. Sullivan

Charles Robb   Samuel Johnson

J. H. Warner

and to their successors legally qualified, to constitute the Union herein named and known under the title of

International Brotherhood of Teamsters

for the purpose of a thorough organization of the trade, and a more perfect Federation of all **Trades** and **Labor Unions**. And the Union being duly formed, is empowered and authorized to initiate into its membership any person or persons in accordance with its own laws. And to conduct the business affairs of said Union in compliance with the best interests of the trade and labor in general. The autonomy of the Union is hereby ordained and secured.

Provided, That the said Union do conform to the Constitution, Laws, Rules and Regulations of the **AMERICAN FEDERATION OF LABOR**, and in default thereof, or any part, this Certificate of Affiliation may be suspended or revoked according to the laws of this **FEDERATION**. And should the said International Brotherhood of Teamsters be dissolved, suspended or forfeit this Certificate of Affiliation, then the persons to whom this Certificate of Affiliation is granted, or their successors, bind themselves to surrender the same with such other property as shall properly belong to this **FEDERATION**. And further, in consideration of the due performance of the above, the

AMERICAN FEDERATION OF LABOR

does hereby bind itself to support the said   International Brotherhood of Teamsters

in the exercise of all its rights, privileges and autonomy as an affiliated Union.

In Witness Whereof, We have subscribed our Names and affixed the **SEAL** of the American Federation of Labor this twenty-second day of August A. D. One Thousand Nine Hundred and Three.

Duplicate Charter

Samuel Gompers   President.

James Duncan   1st Vice-President.

John Mitchell   2d "   "

Jas O'Connell   3rd "   "

Max Morris   4th "   "

Thos. I. Kidd   5th "   "

Denis A. Hayes   6th "   "

EXECUTIVE COUNCIL.

John B. Lennon   Treasurer.

Frank Morrison   Secretary.

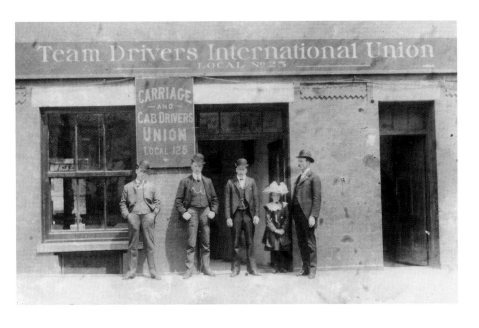

Opposite:
First Charter
The charter for the newly formed International Brotherhood of Teamsters. 1903

Team Driver International Union Local 25
Members of the Team Drivers International Union pose in front of their union hall in Boston. 1899

Traffic Jam
Crowded streets were part of city life for the Teamsters, even before motor trucks appeared on the scene. c. 1906

**D.W. Dunn Co. Packers
& Movers**
Boston. c. 1920

Canadian National Express
Horse-drawn wagons and drivers in Winnipeg.
c. 1916

Delivering Wool
c. 1912

Refrigerated Truck
Delivery of produce and other perishables was greatly improved with new techniques in refrigeration. c. 1923

Eat More Bananas
*Produce delivery truck,
Boston. c. 1918*

Furniture Delivery
*Ira F. Powers Furniture of
Chicago. 1916*

Teamsters Unloading Construction Materials
In 1922, Teamsters were given jurisdiction over loading and unloading materials manually from their trucks at construction sites.

Early Gravel Truck
c. 1918

Early Rigging
Boston Teamsters secure an electric operator onto a flatbed truck to help produce electricity. Connie Bowen Machinery Mover was one of the first Teamster rigging companies in Boston.
c. 1918

Labor Day Parade
*Members of Teamsters
Local 144 in Terre Haute,
Indiana proudly show off
their float in the Labor
Day Parade. 1918*

Opposite:
Happy Anniversary
*Joint Council 26 celebrates
its 25th anniversary.
Cincinnati, Ohio. 1928*

Building Membership:

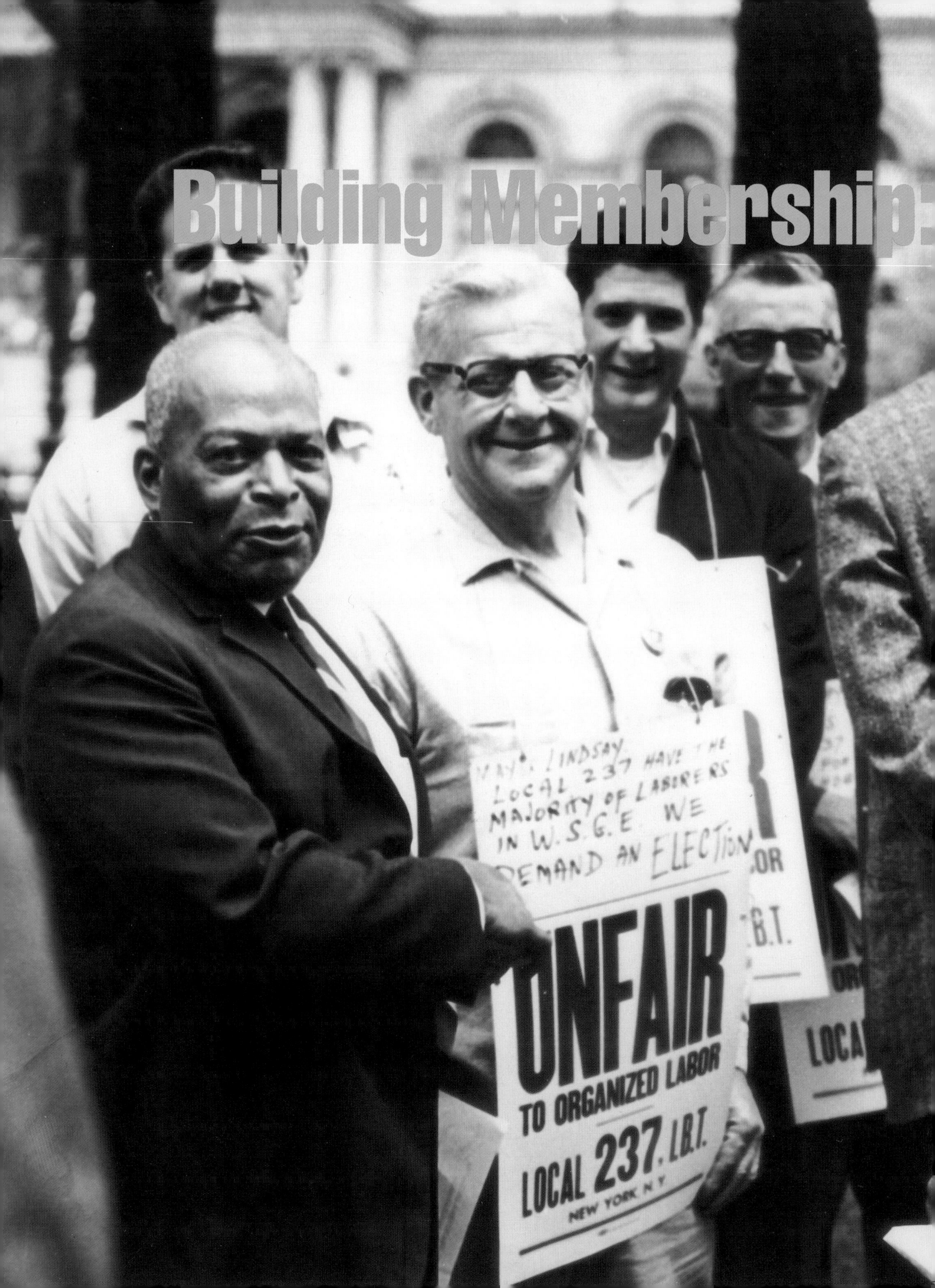

Organizing and Negotiating

Organizing is the lifeblood of all unions. As the labor movement matured in the 20th Century, unions survived or failed based on their ability to achieve critical density in their respective industries.

The odds were stacked against union organizers. As industrialization changed the face of a formerly agrarian nation, the new corporate aristocracy and its allies in legislatures and the courts conspired to prevent the growing ranks of wage-earners from gaining a measure of control over their pay and conditions at work. These powerful forces helped to shape the opinions of a public easily frightened by the prospect of a strike.

For Teamsters, the challenge was particularly daunting. With its traditional workforce largely mobile and vulnerable to exploitation, drivers were easy pickings for employers determined to avoid unions. Yet recognizing the strike as a weapon of last resort, the union used education and training to enhance job security and improve workers' lives.

Off the Hoof, On the Road

An early trial took place in 1905, when the International backed a bloody strike at the Chicago-based Montgomery Ward Company. In the end, Montgomery Ward's cutthroat tactics broke the strike. For the union, which was just two years old, this was a traumatic but effective lesson in the need for solidarity. The following year in the *Teamsters* magazine, Organizer J.E. Longstreet wrote: "If the reader will kindly demand the paid-up monthly button of the Brotherhood of Teamsters' Union—from the coal man, the ice man, the lum-

Fair Warning
A Local 351 striker cautions motorists driving to Simon Fraser University that Teamsters and other unions are actively picketing for a contract. 1967

Opposite:
Strike Duty
Local 237 President William Lewis with members at a 1966 strike.

Expanding the Ranks
Bakery drivers were among the first groups organized by the Teamsters in an effort to expand membership. c. 1906

ber man, the truck man and the hack man, and refuse to be served without it, you will help the overworked and underpaid drivers who will in turn be glad to help others along the same line."

By 1912, the gradual rise of motor traffic and the demise of horse-drawn wagons made obvious the need to adjust tactics in a changing industry. General President Dan Tobin launched a campaign to organize operators of the new technology, bringing into the union beer wagon drivers, gravel haulers and deliverymen for bakers and confectioners.

Although World War I sparked an industrial boom that expanded the transportation sector, the Bolshevik Revolution in Russia helped create a Red Scare used by the government as a pretext for savaging unions in the postwar period. Looking toward the future, Tobin in 1920 sponsored a doubling of the per capita assessment charged to locals, making it possible to raise strike benefits. In addition, the Teamsters expanded their jurisdiction by affiliating with the Canadian Trades and Labour Congress.

Van Drivers Strike
Van drivers on the picket line during the strike in New York City. 1920

The Great Depression

The catastrophic stock market crash of 1929 triggered a chain reaction of misery and despair in North America. As banks collapsed, the jobless rate jumped from 3 percent to 25 percent. By 1933, Teamster membership rolls hit a Depression-era low of 75,000. And as with all economic downturns before and since, employers saw the crisis as an opportunity to bust unions and drive down wages.

In 1934, after a successful strike in the Minneapolis coal yards, Local 574 set up a committee to organize all the transportation workers in the city. With employers refusing to recognize the union, Local 574 struck the city's trucking operations. Some 35,000 building trades workers showed their solidarity by also striking. Although the strike was settled on May 25, employers delayed honoring their commitments, prompting a resumption of the strike on July 16. On July 20—or "Bloody Friday" as it came to be known—police opened fire on strikers, killing two and wounding 55. The governor declared martial law, and the National Guard occupied the Minneapolis local, arresting some 100 officers and members. Because of the ties that had developed throughout the city between the citizens and the Teamsters, a mass march of 40,000 forced the release of the Teamsters and on August 22 the strike was won. "The winning of this strike marks the greatest victory in the annals of the local trade union movement," said the Minneapolis Labor Review

Out of Work
The bleak economic outlook during the depression years left even skilled workers vulnerable to pay cuts and layoffs. c. 1931

Turbulent Times

The violence against workers during the Minnesota Strike of 1934 eventually brought most citizens to the side of the Teamsters. The strike was a successful turning point for organized labor.

of August 24, 1934. "It has changed Minneapolis from being known as a scab's paradise to being a city of hope for those who toil."

The Depression also spurred the union to redouble its efforts to organize the over-the-road trucking industry. The keystone of this organizing approach was the control of truck terminals, from which over-the-road truckers could be organized. By 1935, Teamsters membership stood at 146,000.

War and Peace

During World War II, the Teamsters, like most of organized labor, pledged to refrain from all work stoppages for the duration of the war. Tobin fully subscribed to this policy, maintaining that, "A man who quits work now without the consent and approval of his union—which he cannot get—is and should be and will be classed as an enemy of our nation and of our government." After discussing the subject with British Prime Minister Winston Churchill, Tobin decried "the weak-kneed local officials who should never have been elected to office, and who haven't the red blood in them to take the right stand at the right time."

Following the war, the union made sure that Teamster veterans kept their seniority when they returned to work. By 1949, membership topped one million thanks to organizing in booming post-war industries, including the automotive trades, food processing and dairy industries.

Opening Day
Chicago's South Water Market. 1925

For the Duration
Teamsters aid in promoting strike talks and the idea of "no strikes for the duration" of the war. Thomas Flynn, Local 364 and International staff member talks with Albert Taylor of Local 135. 1942

Congressional passage of the anti-union Taft-Hartley Act in the summer of 1947 boosted management's efforts to reduce labor's influence. In the years immediately following the act, unions saw their right to picket constantly eroded by a succession of court rulings, such as the prevention of Texas Teamsters from picketing an interstate bus company in neighboring Oklahoma. Yet the International continued to perfect its strategy of creating multi-state bargaining units, area-wide negotiations and control of the trucking terminals.

In 1955, a 25-state contract covering all over-the-road and city freight hauling established uniform rates and benefits.

That same year, the Teamsters launched a "have it delivered" campaign aimed at retail shoppers. Other major campaigns for increasing union membership that year included automated vending machine service workers and a successful end to a 16-year strike for recognition by Local 89 at Morgan Packing in Louisville, Kentucky.

These aggressive organizing efforts helped to bolster leverage at the bargaining table, resulting in average hourly wage increases far exceeding those of other unionized transportation and manufacturing workers in the preceding three years. The late 1950s also saw considerable progress in the warehouse industry, with company-paid health insurance and pensions on the bargaining table.

Organizing Macy's Employees
The vote was 98% yes to join Teamsters Local 804. 1948

The World's Largest Union

Despite the AFL-CIO's expulsion of the Teamsters in 1957, the union went on to become the largest union in the world by leading the labor movement in organizing wins. At the same time, the Teamsters developed a legislative and political action component that fought anti-union legislation such as a proposed use of compulsory arbitration to end contract

A Bold Step
The policy committee works on language for the National Master Freight Agreement. 1964

First National Contract
General President James R. Hoffa holds part of the National Master Freight Agreement which was signed in February, 1964.

impasses that would have seriously weakened labor's hand at the bargaining table.

In 1964, the National Master Freight Agreement—the first-ever national agreement in trucking—was the crowning achievement of legendary General President James R. Hoffa. Hoffa strategically worked to establish concurrent expiration dates on all freight agreements so the nationwide unit of drivers could leverage their collective strength to achieve this historical agreement. It covered 400,000 members employed by some 16,000 trucking companies and spawned similar bargaining in other Teamsters trades and crafts. Drivers who had once been at the bottom of the economic ladder saw their strength and power soar as a united group.

Organizing fights in the 1960s were essential to raise standards for all workers, union and non-union alike. An obscure strike by 125 workers at J.M. Blythe Motor Lines in Florida was emblematic of the need to maintain union standards for all 100,000 drivers of refrigerated rigs, including those in the right-to-work South. Salt miners in Detroit improved their representation through Local 283. Dubbing its Piper Cub "The Flying Organizers," Local 147 in Des Moines went airborne to spread the union message across Iowa. Other developments included expansion of the Anheuser-Busch jurisdiction and a national contract in the linen industry.

Reason to Smile
*The National Master
Freight Agreement of 1964
brought more workers
into the middle class than
any other single event in
labor history.*

Flying Organizers
The organizing team from Local 147 found they could save money and time by investing in a plane to travel around their region. 1966

New Challenges, New Opportunities

During a severe recession resulting in part from a huge Vietnam War-derived federal debt, the Teamsters made many advances in the 1970s. In 1976, Teamsters membership topped the two million mark.

But in the 1980s, as the Reagan administration gave the green light to a new deluge of union-busting, the Teamsters faced a unique challenge as trucking deregulation caused a steady decline in membership rolls for the first time since the Depression. And with each passing year, big business lobbyists eroded labor law and took the teeth out of its enforcement. In 1987, the Teamsters re-affiliated with the AFL-CIO.

Much of this pattern continued into the 1990s, despite an economic turnaround during the Clinton years. The union was plagued by financial mismanagement and shrinking resources throughout the 1990s. With morale at an all-time low, major changes were in store that would result in strong contracts and a renewed spirit.

Historic UPS Strike
Teamsters at UPS electrified the nation and provided a shot in the arm to the entire labor movement with their victorious strike. 1997

Strike Support
The coffee truck stops by the picket line to give strikers a break. This and many other types of Teamsters support are common occurrences during labor disputes.
c. 1950

Solidarity
Members of Local 810 rally outside of the Ideal Roller Company plant in Long Island City, New York to show support for the Local 743 election victory at the Ideal plant in Chicago. 1957

Humble/Esso Strike
Christmas gifts and other supplies are brought in for the families of striking workers. 1964

Above:
Proud New Teamsters
Employees of the Superior Scaffold Company show appreciation for their new three-year contract providing wages and benefits enjoyed by other Teamsters. 1968

Left:
NY Telephone
In the early 1960s the Teamsters took on the task of organizing New York telephone employees.

Opposite:
Organizing Cannery Workers
Employees' efforts to join Local 980. c. 1950

DON'T BUY

- ## ESSO
- ## HUMBLE
- ## ENCO
- ## ESSO IMPERIAL

(Standard Oil of New Jersey Products)

Teamsters Local Union No. 391 won an NLRB election and was certified as the exclusive bargaining representative of Gilbarco's 400 employees in Greensboro, North Carolina. The Company, a wholly-owned subsidiary of Standard Oil of New Jersey, refused to bargain in good faith with the Union and committed a multitude of unfair labor practices against its employees. These unfair practices caused the Union to strike on September 23, 1968, and the vast majority of the employees supported this strike. The NLRB is pursuing unfair practice charges against the Company but Gilbarco continues to ignore the law and the rights of its employees.

GILBARCO MANUFACTURERS THE GAS STATION PUMPS FOR THE ABOVE PRODUCTS

GILBARCO   UNFAIR   GILBARCO

PRINTED IN U.S.A.

Consumer Alert
Teamsters encourage all members of the community to join with them in supporting actions against Galbarco Co. and Standard Oil of New Jersey. 1968

Winning Team
The efforts of this Teamster organizing group brought in 1,044 truck drivers and equipment operators employed by the city of Detroit. 1967

Canadian National Railroad
Striking car men demonstrate at the legislative building in Winnipeg. 1914

Milk/Labor Disputes
Men disposing of old, undelivered milk were common scenes during the milk/labor disputes of 1930-31. Employers tried to do their own organizing by offering more money in wages than typical non-union workers earned, but far less than Teamsters.

Opposition to Unions
Police escort scabs in Puerto Rico. 1959

Teamsters in Puerto Rico
Hard work and perseverance brought many new members during the organizing campaign in Puerto Rico. 1959

Vigilant Strikers
Teamster members of Local 676 form a "labor navy blockade" to stop scabs from sneaking into the back of the Armstrong Cork Company by rowboat during the 1965 strike.

"No Tiger in My Tank"
The working slogan for strikers and their supporters during the 1964 Humble/Esso strike.

Crossing the Line
Scabs were brought in by helicopter in an attempt by management to run the refineries during the 1964 Humble/Esso strike.

Victory Smiles
Members of the Linden, New Jersey, Humble Oil plant celebrate as vote returns indicate a Teamster win. 1964

Legislation and Activism

Seeking Justice

W hether through legislation or activism, Teamsters have a rich history of improving conditions for working men and women. Throughout its 100 years, the Teamsters Union has stood up for the rights of all workers through actions in the community, in the workplace and in the halls of Congress.

Since its inception in 1903, the Teamsters has been a political union but it wasn't until later in the century that it found its balance between politics and activism. When the union first began organizing, there were few laws to protect workers' rights. Companies were allowed to use workers as a commodity and referred to them as "employees at will." Organizing in that environment took a special kind of courage. As brave Teamsters fought in the streets against powerful companies, they quickly realized that the government almost always sided with the employer. For that reason, political action was as necessary to the growth of the union as organizing and bargaining.

Although the Teamsters realized the necessity of strong political unity, its first real visibility in Washington took place during Franklin Delano Roosevelt's administration. The union embraced FDR as he fought for working families and won the passage of legislative initiatives to pull the country out of the Depression. And he relied heavily on labor leaders, especially General President Tobin, to make his case.

The crux of FDR's plan to make the country prosperous again was the **National Recovery Act** (NRA). It established minimum wages and maximum hours of labor for each industry. The number of hours employers were allowed to require as work hours were reduced to help shrink the ranks of the

Teamsters actively encourage members to exercise their rights by voting in all elections.

Opposite:
Fighting for Fairness
Teamster wives from North and South Carolina picket the White House in protest of actions affecting union jobs. c. 1961

Service to the Nation
Many Teamsters volunteered for military service after Pearl Harbor in 1941 (above). After the war, veterans like these from Local 843 (below) were anxious to get on with their lives. 1947

unemployed. FDR also won passage of the landmark **National Labor Relations Act of 1935**, which was meant to protect workers in their right to organize and bargaining collectively. The Minnesota Strike of 1934 helped convince those who were reluctant to accept legislation establishing workers' rights and has been credited as the impetus for the legislation.

Canadian Teamsters are governed both by federal and provincial statute. Canadian labor laws have historically been more progressive than those in the United States. After 1935, Canadian workers were guaranteed the right to collective bargaining and to select bargaining agents. A post-war legislative effort produced the Canada Labour Code. Additionally, workers have the right to refuse hazardous work in most jurisdictions. Until recently, Canadian workers were allowed to achieve recognition by simply showing the employer that a majority of the workers wanted union representation.

Protecting Workers

The Great Depression was a difficult time for organized labor, but the NRA helped to restore employment to workers who had been laid off as a result of the economy's crash. The union fought for provisions in the NRA that protected the gains that had been made in the past and, in fact, strengthened the existing rights of unions. As a result, the NRA guaranteed:

- That employees continue to have the right to organize and

to bargain collectively through representation of their own choosing;

- That it was illegal to prohibit an employee from joining a union or to force him to join a company union; and

- That employers had to comply with minimum wage and maximum hour conditions approved or prescribed by the president.

U.S. laws regarding workers address the right to organize, the right to fair and appropriate working conditions, and the right to a measure of security in times of economic stress and during retirement. Much of this legislation was a result of political action by the Teamsters.

The **Railway Labor Act (RLA) of 1926** required employers to bargain collectively and prohibited discrimination against unions. It originally applied to interstate railroads and their related undertakings. In 1936, it was amended to include airlines engaged in interstate commerce.

The **Norris-LaGuardia Act of 1932** prohibited the use of court injunctions as a way of settling labor disputes. It allowed workers the freedom to choose a union to negotiate the terms and conditions of their employment. It also guaranteed work-

Teamsters Back FDR
President Franklin D. Roosevelt with General President Dan Tobin after addressing the 1940 Teamster convention.

Labor Reform
Members of Local 25 in Boston show their support for Roosevelt and labor reform. c. 1944

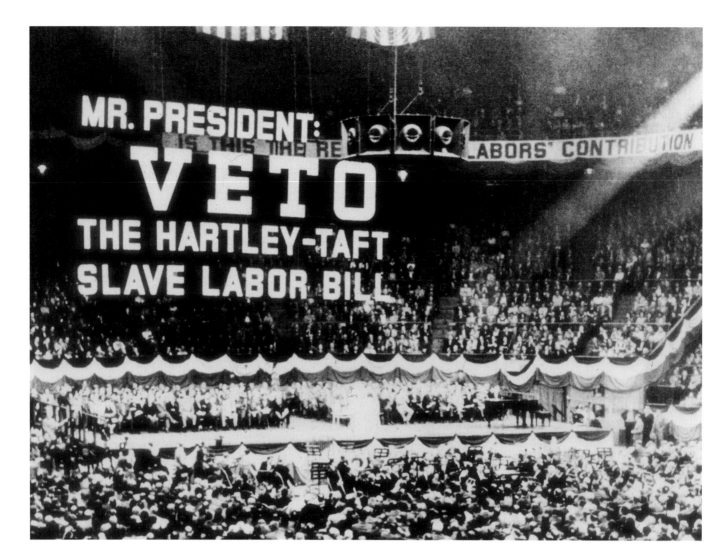

MR. PRESIDENT: IS THIS THE RE... VETO THE HARTLEY-TAFT SLAVE LABOR BILL ...LABORS' CONTRIBUTION

Anti-Labor Legislation

Despite the objections of labor, anti-union sentiment prompted congress to pass the Taft-Hartley Act. Under the Act, secondary boycotts, work stoppages over jurisdictional disputes and the "closed shop" were all outlawed. c. 1947

ers freedom from interference, restraint or coercion on the part of employers or their agents in the designation of union representation.

The **National Labor Relations Act of 1935,** or the Wagner Act as it is also known, afforded security against interference or intimidation aimed against the organizing of labor activities toward collective bargaining. It established the National Labor Relations Board (NLRB). The NLRB's function was to investigate charges and to render decisions on unfair labor practices by employers. Later, the anti-union Taft-Hartley Act of 1947 extended NLRB jurisdiction to include unfair labor practices filed by employers against unions.

The **Social Security Act of 1935** filled many voids that had remained largely vacant until the new law was enacted, including providing old age pensions, health and disability insurance, and unemployment benefits.

The **Fair Labor Standards Act of 1938** established a maximum work week of 44 hours and a minimum hourly wage rate, which at the time was set at 25 cents an hour for employees working in industries dealing with interstate commerce.

General President Tobin said that the act "embodies the fundamental principles" for which labor had fought "with courage and tenacity."

The **Motor Carrier Safety provisions of 1938** established maximum hours of service for drivers and motor vehicles operated by common and contract carriers. In it, the Interstate Commerce Commission ruled on working hours for drivers by virtue of the safety required in their work. After 10 hours of driving, an off-duty period of eight hours was required for each 24-hour working period.

The **Federal-Aid Highway Act of 1956** created the Interstate Highway System. More than any other single act by the U.S. government, the creation of the Interstate Highway System changed the face of America. Its impact on the economy—through the new jobs it would produce in manufacturing, construction and transportation—was phenomenal. It also coincided with a period of dramatic growth for the Teamsters.

The **Occupational Safety and Health Act (OSHA) of 1970** heralded a new era in the history of efforts to protect workers from harm on the job. OSHA established for the first time a nationwide, federal program to protect almost the entire workforce from job-related death, injury and illness.

Local, state and federal government workers in the United States are known as public employees and were often the last workers to achieve organizing and bargaining rights. In the federal government, John F. Kennedy recognized public employees' rights through an Executive Order. Jimmy Carter signed the **Civil Service Reform Act** that granted worker rights under federal law. Most state and local governments modeled workers' organizing and bargaining rights on the RLA and NLRA, with an exception that many states restricted public employees' right to strike.

Legislative Issues
Delegates arrive in Washington, DC for meetings to study anti-labor legislation. 1959

Anti-Worker Legislation

Of course, not every piece of legislation is pro-worker. The union has always kept an eye on Congress and when it tries to sneak in an anti-worker bill, the Teamsters are there to fight for workers. But a massive mobilization of Teamsters and all of

Teamsters National Tour
Speaking out against the Kennedy-Ervin Bill. 1959

Opposite:
DRIVE Goes to Washington
Teamster political activists came to Washington to lobby against anti-labor legislation such as the Taft-Hartley Act. 1965

labor still was not good enough to beat back the **Taft-Hartley Act of 1947.**

With the passage of Taft-Hartley, the authority of the NLRB was extended to handle charges by management on unfair practices. Also known as the Labor-Management Relations Act, the new legislation outlawed jurisdictional strikes, closed shops and secondary boycotts. Further, it allowed the government to obtain an 80-day injunction against strikes under certain conditions.

More anti-union legislation surfaced in the form of the **Labor-Management Reporting and Disclosure Act of 1959,** also known as the Landrum-Griffin Act. The bill required unions to handle struck goods, forcing dedicated union members to act as strikebreakers. The legislation also severely limited use of pickets as organization tools. Additionally, Landrum-Griffin imposed highly complicated legal reporting and disclosure requirements on all unions.

But despite the anti-union legislation being passed, the Teamsters Union continued to grow.

DRIVE to Washington

While the Landrum-Griffin Act was an ominous move on the part of Congress, it spurred the Teamsters to rally together for a common cause. Union officers, as well as the rank-and-file, realized that more effort had to be put into legislative and political activities to protect what had been won at the bargaining table.

DRIVE Committee
Local 776, Harrisburg, Pennsylvania. c. 1966

In 1959, the Teamsters launched **DRIVE**, or **Democrat, Republican, Independent Voter Education**—the political action and legislative arm of the International Brotherhood of Teamsters. DRIVE was born in the aftermath of Landrum-Griffin when it became clear that political and legislative action was required for the survival and prosperity of the union.

"How much more experience do we have to have to realize that we are dead as a labor movement unless we become alive politically?" said Sidney Zagri, Executive Director of DRIVE, in 1963. "It is our responsibility to act, to register to vote, get out the vote, just as management does."

From DRIVE's beginning, Teamsters General President James R. Hoffa had one foot planted under the bargaining table and one foot planted firmly on Capitol Hill. Before passage of Landrum-Griffin, the Teamsters

had always been known as a "bread and butter" union—one that prided itself on negotiating good contracts and enforcing those agreements. After Landrum-Griffin, Hoffa said, "It became very clear to all that what had been gained for the membership in wages, hours and conditions at the bargaining table and on the picket line was being taken away by the political action of our enemies."

Josephine Hoffa, wife of the General President, was the guiding force that initiated the DRIVE program. The October 1963 issue of the *Teamster* magazine had this to say about Mrs. Hoffa: "To the Teamsters movement, she symbolizes the woman in politics to protect economic gains her husband has won at the bargaining table and on the picket line…Jo Hoffa symbolizes the wife of the working man who stepped forward to meet the political challenge of the times and to put DRIVE into ACTION."

Thanks largely to the vision of Josephine Hoffa, DRIVE became America's largest PAC shortly after its inception.

Supporting DRIVE
Members of Local 42 in Lynn, Massachusetts sign up for DRIVE. 1968

Opposite:
Talking Politics
DRIVE activists meet with Vice President Lyndon Johnson to discuss political issues. 1963

Promoting Civil Rights
Members of Local 239 in Little Neck, New York travel to Montgomery, Alabama to join civil rights marchers. They drove 22 hours non-stop to be on time for the rally and march. 1965

Fight for Equality

Dignity in the workplace does not only come from good contracts. It comes from equality—something the Teamsters have fought for from the beginning.

Women's rights. Civil rights. The rights of migrant workers. Child labor. Retiree's rights. These are just a few of the causes taken up in the name of fairness. Through legislation, donations and activism, the Teamsters Union has made more of a difference in these areas than perhaps any union or single organization in North America. Wherever working men and women marched for jobs, civil rights or justice, the Teamsters were on the front lines.

Under the headline, "No Color Line in Teamsters Union," the December 1942 issue of the *Teamster* magazine had this to say: "There is no line, insofar as race is concerned, in our organization."

And the Teamsters practiced what they preached.

In a 1906 issue of the *Teamsters* magazine, there was an impassioned plea for all local unions to organize African-American workers.

"By making an effort to organize them, showing them what organization will do for them, there can be no question but that the colored teamsters of the South will become as much of a power in their locality as the drivers in all other cities where they are organized," the article reads.

The International Brotherhood of Teamsters also championed the cause of women's rights early on. The following was printed in the July 1917 issue of the *Teamsters Journal*: "Equal pay for equal work should become a constant, vigorous slogan among all employees in all crafts. The strength and brains of women and girls are exploited the world over and especially so in the United States. All working men and women should become actively, and, if necessary, drastically interested in

Opposite:
March for Civil Rights
Local 810's delegation to the March on Washington. 1963

Southern Conference of Teamsters
Delegates vote to support civil rights political action. Teamsters were proud of their unsegregated membership in the South. 1959

New Perspectives
Clara Day of Chicago's Local 743 became one of the most prominent women leaders in the union. Here, Day greets civil rights leader Ralph Abernathy. 1968

Opposite:
The Funeral of Viola Liuzzo
In attendance at the funeral were General President James R. Hoffa, Vice President Harold Gibbons, Michigan Teamster leader Bobby Holmes, UAW President Walter Reuther and Dr. Martin Luther King Jr. 1965

fighting for equal pay for duties performed by either sex. The standard of living in every workingman's home is lowered by sexual inequality of pay and both sexes should band together and swat the curse from all parts of the earth where it exists."

In January 1917, the Teamsters won a clause in a contract for women laundry workers that workers would be paid the same regardless of race.

The Teamsters' involvement in social causes was not without consequences. In addition to participating in the historic civil rights event—March to Freedom on August 28, 1963—the Teamsters also adopted a civil rights resolution to contribute money to Dr. Martin Luther King Jr.'s Southern Christian Leadership Conference in 1965. The morning after this resolution and with a heavy heart, General President Hoffa offered a $5,000 reward for the capture and conviction of those who murdered the wife of a business agent from Detroit Local 247.

Viola Liuzzo had been among Teamsters participating in a civil rights march in Alabama. The night of the march, on a stretch of Interstate 80 between Montgomery and Selma, Liuzzo was shot dead by a segregationist. Three years later, King was similarly struck down by an assassin's bullet.

The union continues to strive for political and social jus-

Viola Liuzzo
The wife of Local 247 Business Agent Anthony Liuzzo was murdered while helping transport marchers with Martin Luther King Jr. from Selma to Montgomery, Alabama. 1965

tice. The Teamsters have many different caucuses keeping an eye on inequality in the workplace and in Washington. The International's Human Rights Commission with delegates from three caucuses—the Teamsters National Black Caucus, the Teamsters Hispanic Caucus and the Teamsters Women's Caucus—are all hard at work to support Teamster diversity.

In words and action, the Teamsters have long sought equality for workers regardless of race, sex or age.

Teamsters Take Action
New England Conference of Teamsters sponsored rallies against anti-labor measures. c. 1952

Hear, Hear
Delegates applaud pledges from union leaders to fight increasingly anti-labor legislation. 1947

Rid the nation of this "MENACE"...

Teamsters Opinions
These editorial cartoons are one of the many ways the Teamsters displayed their strong opposition to sections of the Taft-Hartley Act. 1965

**DRIVE Political
Action Committee**
*Enthusiastic DRIVE
activists arrive in
Washington, DC to meet
with legistators. 1965*

Meeting with Dr. King
Joseph Konowe, Director of the Teamsters Industrial Trades Division, talks to Martin Luther King Jr. at a civil rights luncheon held by Governor Nelson Rockefeller in New York. 1964

Mail-in Campaign
Teamsters protest a Defense Department job phase out in Boca Raton, Florida. 1965

Voter Registration
Members of Local 340 in Portland, Maine sponsor a state federated labor board project to register voters. Members are shown with the "mobile registration booth" that was part of the project.
c. 1966

DRIVE in Chicago
Parking workers from Chicago's Local 727 sign up for DRIVE—the Teamsters political action fund. 2002

Solidarity Day, 1991
*New York Teamsters show
their support for labor
issues.*

Anti-NAFTA Rally
Teamsters gather at a rally in Dallas. 2001

Lending a Hand

Community Service and Philanthropy

For 100 years, Teamsters have given back to the communities where they live; helping to improve countless lives and spread hope across North America.

Whether working to increase educational and recreational opportunities for children, fighting for workers' rights, or organizing and sponsoring food and clothing drives for the needy, no history of the Teamsters is complete without highlighting the generosity of the union and its members past and present.

No charity is too big or too small to receive help from the Teamsters. Members have helped local churches and hospitals, and have been active in community health campaigns and blood drives. They have pitched in to make a difference with local organizations, and have given their time and money to large, national charities such as Easter Seals, the March of Dimes and St. Jude's.

One of the hallmarks of the union's community service efforts has been its focus on children. Teamsters have not only raised funds for worthy causes, they have become actively involved with youngsters in their towns. Over the years, many sports teams and scouting groups have received financial support from the union, as well as benefited from the coaching and leadership skills of Teamsters members. Disadvantaged kids and children with health issues have received more than money too. Picnics, camps, recreational clubs, entertainment equipment and specialized vehicles have all been part of the helping hand offered by the Teamsters.

The union's national charity campaigns have reflected this focus as well. Whether it was funds for research facilities,

March of Dimes Day
Sponsored by Local 270 in New Orleans. 1968

Opposite:
To the Rescue
Teamsters were commonly known as "highway helpers" on American roads and interstates. 1959

Teamster Hockey Team
National Bantam Hockey Champions sponsored by Michigan's Local 247. c. 1965

providing quick delivery of a much anticipated vaccine or organizing immunization campaigns, Teamsters have always been there. Giving up a Saturday to volunteer at a hospital, coach a sports team, or take blind children to the beach have all been part of the routine for rank-and-file members.

Human, Worker Rights

In the early years of the Teamsters, the spirit of giving was illustrated by the union's strong, unwavering support of workers who were seeking justice. For example, the Teamsters fought for labor laws to protect children. From the March 1906 edition of the *Teamsters* magazine: "The factory wants the child. There is little to suggest the magic piper in its whistle, yet the summons brings the children scurrying down the broken stairs of poverty and want, and the factory doors close upon them by tens of thousands, leaving their childhood outside." The Teamsters also railed against poverty. "Poverty is the devil's prime minister. It darkens more lives, besots more men, kills more children, beclouds more intellects, quenches more hopes, and inspires more crimes than all other causes combined."

Early in the last century, the Teamsters stressed the importance of education and the need to battle illiteracy. From the October 1919 edition of the *Teamsters* magazine: "Society has not fulfilled its obligation to civilization merely by building schoolhouses, employing teachers, furnishing free books. It

Youth Clubs
Joseph Feraca of Local 602 leads Teamster efforts to plan for the future by working with area youth. 1965

Opposite:
Helping with Health
In 1964, Teamsters from Local 243 volunteer in Detroit's Inoculation Project. The Teamsters donated time and UPS donated trucks to enable vaccines to reach more than two million area residents.

Fighting Child Labor
Child labor was a major concern of the Teamsters from its earliest days. c. 1910

must search out the illiterate man and place within his reach the means of education. He must be given the light."

During the Depression, Teamster members and their families donated clothing and cooked meals for the families of striking and unemployed workers. In short, Teamsters took care of each other during a very difficult time.

Time of War

In times of war, Teamsters generosity rose to new levels. During World War I, it was estimated that four out of five Teamsters purchased liberty bonds.

World War II saw an even greater Teamster effort. The Teamsters offered to give the government an interest-free loan of $8 million from its treasury to help win World War II. President Franklin Roosevelt politely declined the offer, but stated, "(Your offer) should be an example to the whole country."

Supporting the Troops
Many Teamster families purchased war bonds and saving stamps as an aid to the troops. c. 1943

The Teamsters determination to make sure Allied Forces were victorious did not stop there. The union invested 60 percent of its liquid assets in United States bonds during World War II. And it continued to buy bonds as a show of support. Teamsters General President Dan Tobin summed it up: "We weren't fooling when we told President Roosevelt that all of our assets were behind the government in the war and we weren't fooling when we said this war must be won regardless of cost in men and money. The Teamsters are supplying men and money to the limit of their resources."

In addition to buying bonds, Teamsters collected scrap metal for the war effort. For example, 600 members of Local 364 in South Bend, Indiana collected two million pounds of scrap metal from old stoves, fences and other materials that went to the battle fronts in the form of guns, tanks and ammunition.

Teamsters pitched in on the front lines too. When the Japanese bombed Pearl Harbor, a group of Teamsters was put on an Army transport bound for Asia to help in the delivery of supplies along the Burma Road. A week later, some 1,700 Teamsters joined their fellow trade unionists in the Burma Road effort.

Drive to Victory
Teamster families helped the war effort by supporting tire, scrap metal and other drives during World War II. 1943

Helping Refugees
Employees of the Hub Furniture stores aid Joint Council 42 in gathering clothing and supplies for newly arrived refugees. 1957

Helping Israel
Helping the citizens of Israel was a favorite cause of General President James R. Hoffa. The Beth Hoffa orphanage in Israel serves needy children to this day. 1967

Polio, Overseas Assistance

During the postwar years, Teamsters turned to causes such as polio that affected millions of Americans. In July 1950, James R. Hoffa, President of Joint Council 43 at the time, presented a check for $30,306.17 to Clifford R. Tanner of the Wayne County, Michigan chapter of the National Foundation for Infantile Paralysis. The Teamsters check was from the Franklin D. Roosevelt Memorial Ball, sponsored by the union to raise money for the March of Dimes. The check was the largest single contribution received from the drive.

Teamsters also raised money for overseas causes. In 1957, West Coast locals completed a massive clothing drive to assist 200,000 Hungarians who fled to Austria to escape Soviet imperialism. The drive—originally scheduled for ten days—was extended to accommodate the overwhelming response. Donations overflowed all available warehouses and prompted the Teamsters committee to rent additional warehouses in Pasadena for more than 60 tons of clothing.

When Hurricane Audrey swept across Louisiana in 1957—killing more than 500 people—Teamsters sprung into action. Members converged from across North America with their trucks and disaster units to aid in whatever way possible. Volunteers from Local 626 in California worked with meat-packers to load 10,000 pounds of fresh meat onto a truck and

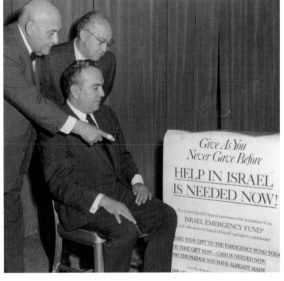

Opposite:
Shipping the Cure
Teamsters aided in rushing the polio vaccine to numerous cities within days of the April 13, 1955 announcement that a successful formula had been found. Teamster warehouseman Peter Golabek applies rush labels to packages of vaccine. 1955

81

drove it to the victims. Teamsters have also risen to the occasion during floods, especially involving the Ohio River disasters.

Relief Efforts
Over 400 families of Teamsters were affected by the flood from Hurricane Betsy in 1965. Teamsters at Local 270 were among the first to help with relief efforts in Florida and Louisiana.

*Below:
Teamsters re-locate tornado victims.*

Social Justice

The 1960s brought a new era of giving—especially involving social justice. In April 1961, Local 299 in Detroit and University of Michigan students collected four tons of food and clothing for the evicted sharecroppers in the Haywood and Fayette counties of Tennessee. General President Hoffa announced that Teamster locals across the country would help to provide food and clothing to the families at "Freedom Village" who were being punished for registering to vote and voting in the 1960 election. "There are about 700 black fami-

lies who are living in crude tents and have been faced with virtually a total economic boycott since the November elections," Hoffa said.

Teamsters giving doesn't always involve raising money. Sometimes, just showing up for a cause and marching made the difference. On August 28, 1963, thousands of Teamsters were among the more than 200,000 persons taking part in the historic March to Freedom in Washington, D.C. Members from Locals 239, 743, 810, 875 and many others, participated in the famous civil rights march. The march developed into the greatest, and possibly most significant peaceful demonstration in the history of the nation culminating in Dr. Martin Luther King Jr.'s famous "I Have A Dream" speech.

Supporrting Fairness
Top: Members of Local 97 check over supplies sent to civil rights activists who marched from Selma to Montgomery, Alabama. 1965

Above: Local 688 aids families of unemployed workers. 1958

Fighting Disease
James R. Hoffa gets aquainted with Cystic Fibrosis poster child Joanna Everett as part of the Teamster campaign to fight the disease. 1966

Opposite:
Knowledge for a Lifetime
The James R. Hoffa Memorial Scholarship Fund makes continued education a possiblitly for all Teamster children. 2003

Recovery Effort
Teamsters participated in the recovery efforts at the Oklahoma City bombing site. 1995

1970s to Today

During the 1970s, Teamster generosity didn't let up. For example, an annual golf tournament raised more than $100,000 each year for physically and mentally challenged children and young adults who reside at Little City in Palatine, Illinois. Teamsters also helped another favorite charity—International Guiding Eyes—which provides dogs for the sightless. A banquet in Los Angeles in 1975 raised more than $100,000 for the charity.

Today, the spirit of Teamsters giving is stronger than ever. From fund-raising by the Teamster Horseman Motorcycle Association, a 500-member organization that has raised more than $50,000 to fight multiple sclerosis, to Local 938's $19,500 gift to a Toronto, Ontario women's shelter, Teamsters are giving more than ever.

Other examples include donations to the Boy Scouts of America, which was strongly supported by James R. Hoffa and his son, James P. Hoffa. Teamsters locals also participate in charity walks, including Local 853's walk to cure multiple sclerosis, which has raised more than $140,000 with over 90 local unions and Joint Councils participating. The

International Brotherhood of Teamsters
2003–2004 Academic Year Scholarships

Knowledge *for a* Lifetime

THE JAMES R. HOFFA MEMORIAL SCHOLARSHIP FUND

For High School Seniors who are
Children of Teamster Members

For more information, contact your
local Teamsters union office or visit www.teamster.org

Delivering Hope
Teamsters respond in the wake of the September 11, 2001 attacks.

marchers are known as the TeamMSters.

Members continue to donate to the union's Disaster Relief Fund which assists union members whose lives are turned upside-down. As of December 2002, more than $700,000 had been distributed to assist families.

Teamsters have also generously donated money to the James R. Hoffa Memorial Scholarship Fund. The scholarship winners use the money to further their education, as well as the legacy of the Teamsters. Each year, 75 scholarships are awarded. Applicants compete in one of five geographic regions where their Teamster parent or grandparent's local union is located. Currently, 25 of the awards total $10,000 each. Fifty of the awards are one-time grants of $1,000.

Following the September 11, 2001 terrorist attacks, Teamsters responded in many ways: Truck drivers donated their time to cart away debris, locals raised money for victims' families and the union coordinated a delivery of communications equipment vital to the World Trade Center disaster relief effort.

Once again, Teamsters came through in a crisis—one of the biggest ever.

Building Dreams
Teamsters volunteer with Habitat for Humanity in Washington, DC. 1996

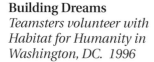

Ground Zero
General President James P. Hoffa and fellow Teamsters survey the damage where the World Trade Center once stood. 2001

Sponsoring Youth Groups

Teamsters community outreach efforts to local youth included sponsoring scout troops, Indian Guides and athletic teams. Locals 999 and 945 with Indian Guides. 1964

Wave of the Future

Teamsters "Space Pilots" man this Luer Packing Company "ship to the moon." The traveling vehicle provided educational material and demonstrations about space travel to schoolchildren. 1958

Protecting Communities
Teamsters were active in efforts to protect their communities from natural disasters as well as hostile attacks. Local 59 Civil Defense Unit. 1942

Donating Blood
Members of Local 102 in Newark, New Jersey filled three buses chartered by the union for volunteers to cross the river into New York City to give blood. Red tape had prevented a mobile unit from coming to the plant. 1958

Opposite:
Aiding Earthquake Victims
Teamsters in Allentown, Pennsylvania send supplies to Seward, Alaska earhquake victims. Members from a number of locals across North America helped make the drive in shifts. 1964

"Operation Death Trap"
Teamsters in Bridgeton City, New Jersey participate in "Operation Death Trap" to remove old and abandoned refrigerators around the city. 1968

Teamster Volunteers
Teamsters from Locals 607 and 282 serve as volunteers on the Nesconset, Long Island Ambulance Crew. 1968

Protecting Our Own
Teamsters Joint Councils and local unions helped strikers at the Blythe Motor Company by adopting a family at $75 a week. In addition, some health care benefits were provided by the International. 1966

Bestowing Honors
Teamsters from Local 945 in Clifton, New Jersey honor Tscherim Soobzokou who helped more than 1,000 refugees find work upon their arrival in the United States. 1966

Magic Flute
Teamsters from Local 364 employed at the Gemeinhardt Flute Company in Elkhart, Indiana made a special flute for a young girl from New Mexico. She desperately wanted to play the instrument but could not due to a missing finger from an accident. 1967

Merry Christmas
Teamsters from Local 445 in Newburgh, New York donate food and Christmas gifts to needy families. 1958

Atoms for Life
General President Dave Beck and fellow Teamsters present cobalt isotopes to the City of Hope National Medical Center to fight leukemia. 1955

Day in the Park
General President William McCarthy joins school children on the slide as part of a community outreach program in Washington, DC. 1989

Stamping Out Diabetes
General President James P. Hoffa and hundreds of Teamsters volunteers participate in the "Walk to Cure Diabetes" event for the Juvenile Diabetes Foundation. 2003

Adapting to Change

Broadening the Teamsters Horizons

"*Labor must keep abreast of progress. Labor cannot and does not expect to hold back the clock. Our job is to work for the best interests of employees in a constantly changing industry.*"

– Frank J. Gillespie, Local 754

In the decades before and after Gillespie shared these thoughts in 1952, the Teamsters practiced that very philosophy, which has allowed the union to thrive for a century.

One of the union's strongest qualities is that although it began as an organization of team drivers, it has changed and expanded over time to address the needs of its members and workers. In the process, the union has attracted new members from industries far outside its original ranks.

Over the last century, the union has proven itself extremely adaptable. Teamsters have seen the very fabric of their lives altered by technology. These changes necessitated the emergence of energetic, imaginative leaders to guide the union with a solid vision for the future and skill at keeping pace with advances in every field of labor.

The first major adjustment for the Teamsters came early in the life of the union. Just a few years after the formation of the International Brotherhood of Teamsters, use of the motorized vehicle began creeping into everyday life. This one-time curiosity and toy of the rich suddenly threatened the livelihood of members employed to haul and deliver goods by horse and wagon.

General President Tobin recognized that the "motor truck" was the wave of the future for transporting goods. He

All in a Days Work
A Teamsters driver waits to move on as "residents" of the area cross the road. c. 1930s

Opposite:
Moving Up
Tony Maiton, a 38-year Teamster veteran, works as an aisle ranger at the Star Market. c. 1980s

The Union Service Card
Proudly carried and displayed by members at a wide variety of shops and businesses, this card shows the 1940 official name change to include Warehousemen in the title.

knew ignoring the situation would weaken the union and leave workers vulnerable and unprepared to cope with the rapidly changing world. He created an aggressive plan to organize workers at the fledgling motor truck companies and give them a place under the Teamster banner. He also worked hard with companies that were shifting from horses to motor power to ensure the transitions were gradual enough to allow workers to adjust and learn new skills.

Driving Into a New Era

Cross Country Journey
The first transcontinental delivery by motor truck marked a new era for the Teamsters. 1912

In 1912, Teamsters from the Charles W. Young Company in Philadelphia drove off on a mission that would not only change the very basis of the union, but would earn a place in the industrial history of the United States.

The Teamsters drivers set out from Philadelphia with three tons of Parrot Brand Olive Oil Soap, and headed for Petaluma, California. By the time they reached their destination they had caught the attention of the country and set a historic precedent. This first transcontinental delivery by motor truck would serve as the inauguration of a new era in the transportation of merchandise.

This was an exciting time—full of possibilities for the future—with one regrettable downside for Teamsters. The horses, or "teams" that had been the

National Parks Transcontinental Highway
Demonstration trip under auspices of
SEATTLE CHAMBER OF COMMERCE
Delivering one ton
Carnation Milk
Made in Washington
FROM SEATTLE · TO NEW YORK
DISTANCE 3640 MILES · IN 30 DAYS
GMC TRUCK

GMC · Carnation
GOLDEN PACEMAKER RUN
SEATTLE · NEW YORK · LOS ANGELES

Above:
Milk Delivery
This transport of Carnation products from Seattle to New York took over 30 days. 1916

Left:
50 years later, the Golden Pacemaker Run with Carnation products took six days, and that included a return trip to Los Angeles. 1966

faithful and trusted companion of the drivers, came to the end of their road. The Teamsters would show an ability to adapt to numerous changes over the coming decades, but through an almost unspoken agreement amongst the ranks, one thing would never change. The horse would always be a proud and lasting symbol for the members, honoring the heritage and traditions that gave rise to a great union.

A Turning Point for Labor

Tensions had begun to rise in Minnesota as strikers and police faced off in 1934.

A Pivotal Time

After World War I, numerous advances in technology quickened the pace of America's move into the "modern age." These changes affected workers in almost every industry. Teamsters had originally worked for local cartage or delivery based on city businesses. As companies expanded, their markets expanded beyond city boundaries. Drivers were increasingly needed for what came to be known as "over-the-road" or long distance deliveries. At the time, "over-the-road" drivers were considered unskilled and were forced to work for low wages in poor conditions. They were not protected by the benefits of a union and, in fact, most unions were wary of taking these workers on as members.

These new drivers, many located in cities such as Detroit and Minneapolis, were becoming increasingly frustrated with their situation and began tentative attempts to organize and become part of a union. Their attempts were not very successful. Employers often formed groups among themselves and joined with influential community leaders to make sure that workers stayed unorganized. Minneapolis in particular was openly hostile to organized labor and had such a group named the "Citizens' Alliance." Conditions in Minneapolis reached a point where angry workers were forced to take action. Encouraged by pro-labor provisions in Roosevelt's National

Recovery Act, the truckers decided in the spring of 1934 to challenge the city's anti-labor stance.

At the same time, Teamster leaders in the region realized that the union needed to organize "over-the-road" drivers in order to maintain their strength in the labor movement. Tobin and the other leaders at the International, after much debate, offered some assistance to Local 574 members in Minneapolis who—acting on behalf of the workers—demanded improved working conditions and recognition of the union as their bargaining agent. The negative response of the city's employers and government officials led to a trucker's strike that shut down the city. Special deputies were enlisted to force truckers back on the road to no avail. Building trades workers went on strike in support of the truckers and tensions rose. Increasingly violent confrontations occurred, culminating in a May riot that rocked the city for two days, leaving hundreds injured and several dead. In the aftermath, the tide began to turn in favor of the strikers. Some tentative agreements were reached, only to be broken a short time later by employers in the city. The strikers marshaled forces again, leading to another violent confrontation in July. This time however, the strikers prevailed with many of their demands being met.

The Minneapolis strike of 1934 is widely seen as a pivotal moment for the Teamsters and the labor movement. For the Teamsters, its membership increased as the barriers against "non-craft" workers were eased, and the union's stature as a powerful force in the labor movement increased. The outcome of the strike also led to the enactment of legislation acknowledging the rights of workers to organize and bargain.

Martyred in Minnesota
Violence continued to escalate during the 1934 strike, leading to the death of two Teamsters shot in the back by police in July.

Vending Machines
This industry experienced major growth during the 50s and 60s and added thousands of members to the Teamsters. 1967

Strip Mining for Copper
Major construction projects galvanized the Building Materials and Construction Trades Division of the union. 1956

A Changing World

Jurisdictional disputes among various unions in the years immediately following World War I also brought changes to the membership. In 1922, after many debates, the Teamsters were given jurisdiction over materials unloaded from trucks at docks and waterfront storage areas with longshoremen maintaining control over goods loaded and unloaded off of ships. In a separate decision the same year, the Teamsters were granted control over materials unloaded manually at construction sites. Several years later, in 1928, the Teamsters affiliated with the Building Materials Division of the AFL, creating the Building Material and Construction Trades Division.

The number of warehouse-related employees had been growing steadily over the years just as the use of stables had passed. In 1940, the Teamsters officially became known as the International Brotherhood of Teamsters, Chauffeurs, Warehousemen, and Helpers of America to reflect the changing nature of the members' jobs.

Growth of the membership dropped during the Depression years due to industry hardships and subsequent unemployment, but the Teamsters did not lose their motivation for organizing new members. The concept of Joint Councils and area conferences was introduced during this time, and these innovations helped strengthen the organizing capability of the union. The onset of World War II placed membership on the upswing again with a significant number of women becoming Teamsters as men were sent overseas to fight. The Teamsters also fought to allow African-American workers to take jobs traditionally held by whites.

Innovative technologies and changes in lifestyle during and after World War II created new industries and new opportunities to organize. Food processing, cannery and vending machine trades would all experience great growth in mid-century and swell the ranks of the union even further.

Safety Standards
Top: Teamsters worked hard to bring safety standards to the food processing industry. 1959

Cream of the Crop
Above: The area of food processing had grown considerably by the 1950s. Here, Local 471 workers complete the packaging of Land O'Lakes butter. 1954

Early Carhauler
South Bend, Indiana.
Local 364. 1939

Managing Growth

The Freight Division—always the backbone of the Teamsters—continued to grow, but also faced challenges after the war. The amount of freight handled by Teamsters had grown so rapidly that a decision was reached to divide it into smaller, more manageable units. Sections of the freight industry split into separate divisions within the union and were named after the primary products being hauled. The new divisions—Tankhaul, Carhaul and the Parcel and Small Packages Division—allowed for a more specialized form of bargaining and representation. The Freight Division was also the catalyst for organizing efforts in support industries such as garage and service station employees.

One of the challenges faced within the Freight Division was providing employment for all of its members. Returning veterans were guaranteed maintenance of their seniority in an effort to assure them jobs upon their return home. However, a new generation of workers coming of age and an increased number of

Opposite:
Truck Checks
Instituted in 1950, this truck check took place in San Francisco by Local 85. 1955

people flocking to the cities from rural America created a tight job market. A creative and heavily promoted "Have It Delivered" campaign was developed to help provide more jobs.

Another challenge faced by Teamsters in the postwar years were poor highway conditions coupled with the increasing number of independent "gypsy" drivers taking to the roads, causing numerous hazards. In response to these issues, the Teamsters became leaders in the area of safety and training. A wide variety of comprehensive training programs were designed, along with national safety awareness drives. As a result, the Teamsters gained the reputation as "highway helpers." National truck checks were instituted as well, engineered to "stop everything that rolled" to determine whether contractors and owners of goods were abiding by all labor-management agreements. This truck check system also helped ferret out the non-union drivers who were causing havoc on the highways.

Safety First
Teamsters always recognized and promoted the importance of safe driving. Members of Local 493 in Connecticut receive awards for their efforts, one of the many award-winning Teamster safety projects through the years. 1967

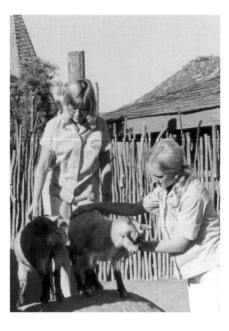

Airline Mechanic
These workers became part of the Teamsters in the early 1960s.

Wild at Heart
San Diego Zoo Wild Animal Park employees, all Teamsters, tend their charges. 1973

Teamsters A-to-Z

The transition to representing employees in the airline industry was a natural one. A union based on representing transportation and transportation service workers in the freight industry was a natural fit for the newest and fastest growing transportation industry in the country.

The Teamsters began organizing the airline industry in the early 1960s, with the Airline Division being officially established in 1961. At the same time, the Bakery, Brewery and Soft Drink divisions were becoming firmly established while the Dairy, Industrial Trades and Canadian Conference of Teamsters developed in the ensuing decades. By the end of its first century, the Teamsters had become a truly multifaceted, diverse organization. A Teamster can honestly boast that their union has members in every field of endeavor, running the gamut from airline mechanics to zoo keepers.

The Teamsters has not only survived changes in technology but also learned to use it to its advantage. Recognizing the power of television, the Teamsters took a chance and broadcast their 16th Annual Convention in 1952 so more members could participate in the event and their

Gas Station Attendants
Local 639 Teamsters demonstrate their support as employees of the first "union shop card" station in the area. 1959

Kansas City Docks
*Teamsters load trucks
with goods taken off rail
cars. 1954*

union. That same spirit is still in place today. The development of the Internet has been a major revolution in communications technology and the union is determined to use it well. The Internet is currently being used to provide up-to-date information to the membership on health and safety issues, government regulations and legislation, contract campaigns, important union news and events, as well as serving as a valuable organizing and educational tool.

The labor movement will keep experiencing growing pains with industrial and technological advances into the 21st Century. But in the spirit of Local 754's Frank J. Gillespie, the International Brotherhood of Teamsters will continue to keep abreast of progress while working for the best interests of working men and women everywhere.

Training New Drivers
Teamsters from Local 261 in New Castle, Pennsylvania train new drivers as part of a co-op with the State Manpower Act. 1965

International Education
Local 815 members expanded their knowledge at a Teamster-sponsored seminar at the London School of Economics. 1966

Job Training
*Instructor Ed Cucchiarello
explains the fine points
of an ascilloscope motor
as part of the "Transpor-
tation Opportunity
Program" job training
sponsored by Joint
Council 42. 1968*

Coal Handlers
One of the original crafts to be represented by the Teamsters, a member of Local 364 in Indiana shovels coal down the chute on one of his many stops for the Feaser Coal Company. 1938

Cannery Row
In food processing, a National Conference of Fruit, Vegetable and Produce Industries was formed to cover employees in canneries and the new frozen food packing companies. c. 1952

The Oil Man
A Teamster readies his Studebaker truck to make deliveries. Teamsters evolved from the coal wagon to the oil truck. The Studebaker truck was used frequently in oil deliveries. 1940

UPS Driver
c. 1970

Putting Food on the Table
*An employee demonstrates
agility and balance as she
harvests mushrooms grown
in an abandoned mine.*
1955

Soft Drink Driver
Portland, Oregon. 1971

Car Rental Workers
In the 1960s, Teamsters membership expanded to include companies such as National Car Rental. National employees in Detroit were pleased with their first contract signed in 1968.

Heavy Machinery
Maria Brandon of Local 786 in Elmhurst, Illinois stands by the heavy duty equipment she works with every day.
c. 1980s

Medical and Rescue Workers
At the scene of an accident. c. 1973

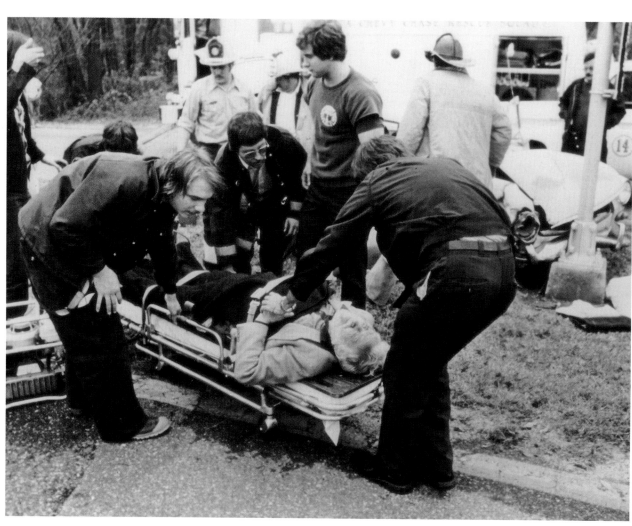

**Motion Picture
Teamsters**
On the set. 1979

Teamsters at Work

In 1954, Zeberdee Barnes was making 50 cents an hour as a "car hiker"—a valet parking cars in Chicago.

While his job routine didn't change a whole lot over 42 years, his life did. When the Teamsters secured his first contract later that same year, Barnes's salary more than doubled to $1.15 an hour.

"Over the years, the benefits got better and better and better," said Barnes, who is now Vice President of Local 727 in Chicago. "The Teamsters changed my life. I was given a chance to have a voice in the workplace and get decent wages and benefits so that I could afford to send my children to college."

As the union celebrates its 100th anniversary, stories like Zeberdee's can be found in every Teamster industry.

Many Faces, One Union

When it all began, members used carts, wagons and the all-important horse to drive North America's economy.

The union's roots lie with team drivers and warehouse workers or what was known originally as "stablemen." But what makes the Teamsters so unique is their diversity.

Today's Teamsters perform a wide array of work outside of the union's original craft. Unlike unions that represent workers from a single craft or industry, Teamsters work in all types of occupations and industries.

Teamsters are public employees and industrial plant workers, health care professionals such as nurses and laboratory technicians, dairy and food processing workers, brewery and laundry employees, truck drivers, warehouse workers and airline mechanics. Teamsters drive equipment to and from

Proud to be Teamster
Teamsters found ways to show their pride in addition to their membership pins. Many locals became very creative with their use of buttons, hats, banners and stickers.

Opposite:
Union Service
Drivers would only patronize service stations that display the union service sign. 1950

117

Food Delivery
Teamsters working in food delivery for the F. C. Schilling Co. of Green Bay, Wisconsin. 1910

movie sets, deliver and sort packages, practice law, keep communities safe while working as police officers, corrections officers and firefighters, and perform as Mickey Mouse and Donald Duck at Disney resorts—bringing smiles to millions of children each year. Those are just some of the "Teamster" occupations.

From the beginning, the Teamsters Union has raised workers' standards of living and position in society, bringing millions into the middle class. The union has provided hope to those who otherwise would have faced poverty.

Garbage Hauler
Oregon. c. 1910

Union Legacy

In 1906, AFL President Samuel Gompers addressed the Teamsters' Convention, summing up the union's legacy.

"Ten years ago, there was no organization among the teamsters of the country, and the driver was treated with less consideration by his employer than the horse he drove. The horse was petted and well fed, while the driver and his family often went without the

Delivering the Goods
Early Teamsters making a dry goods delivery.
c. 1907

necessities of life. The International Brotherhood of Teamsters has changed all this, and has bettered the condition of the teamsters all over the country. The horse continues to be well treated, and the drivers' demand for consideration is now respected."

Teamsters tasks have changed over the years. Along the way, the union has made sure that members work under better conditions, have better equipment and that their rights are protected. Strong contracts have addressed those issues and the union has also fought for laws to protect workers.

The average working day for a typical rank-and-file member has changed considerably since 1903. In the early days, much emphasis was focused on taking care of the "equipment." A poorly fed and tired horse could delay deliveries and ultimately limit a driver's wages. Everyone, regardless of occupation or class, had some interaction with horses and wagons on a daily basis.

The Truck Arrives

This changed with the arrival of the "motor truck." Teamsters with years of experience suddenly had to learn a new way to do an old job. A driver now had to have clear knowledge of the best route where roads would be safe, places to get fuel, possible weather hazards that might affect the motor or handling of the vehicle and how to complete any number of repairs. Teamsters had always been subjected to adverse conditions, but the early drivers faced "problems within problems" related to weather and roads. Rainy days did more than make a driver damp and miserable. Water in the engine could cause

New Rig
Two Teamsters prepare to make deliveries for S. Thompson Co. in Oregon.
c. 1925

it to stall out, and rubber tires were much less "sure footed" on the road than a horse.

Trucks were equipped with simple heaters for cold weather, which was a step up from the lap robe, but offered little true comfort, a situation that was not remedied until many years later. Countless drivers recall driving with one hand on the wheel and the other warming up in a coat pocket. Most drivers could also show off smooth, hairless knees and calves, because a very hot engine with no protective barrier singed their legs on a daily basis. And drivers were still responsible for the care of the "equipment" even though four tires had replaced four hooves.

Beer Delivery
Brewery delivery truck, Detroit. c. 1918

Warehouse workers were often only paid when goods were being loaded or unloaded; yet they were required to wait hours for trucks to arrive. Retail and catalog warehouse workers had to memorize many stock items and catalog numbers, and could expect to walk many miles to fill orders in the course of a shift—all for very low pay and little or no say in procedures or assignments.

Women found that they not only had to do the job, but had to spend as much time proving they could do it. Once they did prove themselves capable, some found this only led to scorn and ridicule. African-American Teamsters may have found no color line within the union hall, but on the job was another matter. Pay was the same due to contracts, but attitude and behavior could not be closely governed by an agreement. Highly skilled workers were given tasks more appropriate for a novice, and advancement, if it happened at all, took much longer than for their white counterparts.

All Teamsters had some things in common on an average day. They were expected to be at work, on time, with a neat appearance and decent attitude. These expectations came not from the employer but the union and, most notably, themselves. Members

Business as Usual
Haymarket Square in Boston. c. 1930

Ice Man Cometh
Harry Young, Local 221, delivers ice in Minneapolis. 1954

121

Well-Dressed Teamsters
Standing with their trucks for a company photo. Yellow Transit Co. c. 1935

Go Fish
Teamsters Betty Sprague and Claire Brown from Local 638 clean fish at the Lyon Fish Co. in Minneapolis. 1954

Casting a Ballot
During the organizing campaign at Macy's by Local 804. 1947

knew that being a Teamster meant respect and dignity in the workplace, and an equal voice in the community, all of which had to be earned.

Regaining What Was Lost

As the Teamsters Union closes its first century, organizing new members is more important than ever. Frank Fosco, a part-time organizer at Local 705 in Chicago, worked in the "piggy-back" yards from 1972 until the mid-1990s. Piggy-back yards are where truck trailers are loaded onto or off of trains. Over the years, the job changed due to innovations, which resulted in double stacking of trailers.

"It got busier and busier," Fosco said. "And it's not an easy job. You're working out in the cold all day."

Most of the piggy-back yards were Teamster-represented in the 1960s and '70s, but the union lost members in the 1980s and '90s. With dedicated union men like Fosco organizing, that trend is being reversed.

"I'm helping to regain what we lost," said Fosco, who has helped organize hundreds of new members. "I want to see the guys walk away after 30 years like I did, with a good Teamsters pension."

Big Changes

Over the decades, many Teamsters jobs changed dramatically. An article appearing in the *Teamster* magazine in 1965 offered an example of how far working men and women have come since the early years of the 20th Century. The article's focus was John Conroy, a milkman from 1912 to 1965:

If one has been a milkman since 1912, several things stand out in memory. First, one spent many hours with reins in one's

Parking Worker
At System Auto Parking Garage in Phoenix, Arizona, a Local 274 member checks out customers. c. 1954

The Milk Man
Before the creation of the supermarket, the milk man delivered products to the doorstep. Here, Clifford Peterson of Local 471 delivers dairy products for Northland Milk Company. 1954

The Gas Man
Walter Pool of McKales Inc. making a delivery to one of the firm's organized service stations. 1954

The Pepsi Challenge
Monitoring all the stages in the bottling process at the Pepsi-Cola plant in Baltimore. c. 1955

hands true Teamster style, before the advent of motor power and the steering wheel. Secondly, one handled 12.5 million bottles of milk, to say nothing of countless units of butter, cheese, cream, and other dairy items. Thirdly, if one were an enlightened milkman, one spent many, many years as a union member, striving to improve wages, hours, and working conditions.

Those things come to mind if one was an ordinary milkman for 52 years. But, if one were like John Conroy of East Chicago, Indiana, those were routine considerations among

Hooking Up
A Teamster driver attaches a second trailer to his rig. c. 1974

"Pretty" Teamster
Shirley Roe, of Local 214 was named Detroit's "Prettiest Meter Maid" in the 1970s.

From the Ground Up
*Teamsters at work on a
large construction site.
1977*

other achievements. Conroy, recently retired, has been a
Teamster for 47 years, and for the last 10 years has been a
trustee of Local 835.

Conroy began when he was 11 years old as a helper, along a
route crisscrossing over dirt roads. He would meet his driver at
3:30 a.m., work until 8 a.m., change clothes, go to school, then
return to the dairy to feed and clean the horses. All this earned
him $1 a week, which went to his mother, a widow, to help pro-
vide for the family. When Conroy was 16, he was taken on as a
regular driver, at the rate of $18 per week. It was a 365-day- a-
year job, no vacation, no holidays, no health and welfare, and
no pension.

In compiling a perfect record of making
deliveries despite the elements, Conroy often
switched from a wagon to a sled during the
winter months. He even waded through deep
snow on Easter morning 1920 to get the
products to customers.

Conroy has had an active life, including
meeting five U.S. Presidents during the course
of his local political career, but Conroy is
quick to point out that he was able to support
his full and active life on the wages of a milkman because of the support of the Teamsters.

Meeting With Members
*A Teamster steward meets
with members of his
Washington, DC local.
c. 1965*

Risking Life and Limb
Jesse Graham of Local 977 risked his life to save another truck driver by pulling him from his burning rig. 1965

Funeral of Charles McCombs
McCombs, from Local 526, lost his life while attempting to save a Massachusetts state trooper. 1967

Above and Beyond

One thing that has set Teamsters apart is their ongoing efforts to go above and beyond the call of duty. It is not unusual for on-the-job Teamsters to stop and help out people in need.

In 2003, a Teamster whose job is to help stranded motorists on the Massachusetts Turnpike went well beyond the call of duty, running into oncoming traffic and jumping into a moving vehicle driven by a woman who apparently suffered a seizure. This brave action averted what could have been an enormous tragedy.

Paul McArthur, a 14-year Local 127 member from Quincy, Massachusetts, played down his act of heroism.

"I did what anyone else would have done," said McArthur, 39, who works for the Turnpike Authority. "You don't have time to think—you just respond and react. I'm glad nobody was seriously hurt."

Back in the 1950s, Teamster Herbert Hayes stayed with his truck when its brakes failed, making sure the 20-ton cargo of copper wire didn't career into other drivers on a California highway. Hayes remained in his truck rather than jump out of

the cab, which cost him his life when the truck eventually jumped an embankment and plummeted 384 feet off a cliff.

The heavily loaded truck endangered other truckers and motorists, but Hayes stayed in the cab, sounding his horn and flashing his lights as a warning to let others know of his desperate plight.

In 2001, Teamster Bill Moore's morning began the same as any other day—waiting for coffee in the drive-thru lane at Dunkin' Donuts.

But Moore, a mechanic for the New York State Thruway Authority, noticed something strange on the ground floor of a nearby building. Through a window, he saw flames dancing up a curtain. On the second floor, he could see people unaware of the blaze below.

"I didn't think about it, I just knew there were people in the building that needed to get out," said Moore, an 11-year member of Local 72. "My adrenaline was pumping. I climbed through a window and started rousting people from the apartments upstairs."

Moore made three trips into the burning building. By the time he was done, all 20 residents were safely evacuated and his lungs were in spasm from the smoke.

When the fire department arrived, Moore caught his breath and headed to work.

Rising Tide
Teamster Dave Brown of Local 448 checks damage to his truck from flash flood waters west of Maria's Pass on the Continental Divide. Brown rescued 21 other motorists during the flood. 1964

No Brakes
Paul Horodeski (left) and Vito DeRosa used skill and quick thinking to safely ride out the loss of their brakes in 1968. Less trained and alert drivers could have turned the episode into tragedy.

Making Daily Deliveries
c. 1906

Keeping It Clean
Teamsters keep fleet in good working order.
c. 1930s

Rolling Kegs
Two Teamsters employed by Knickerbocker's Beer roll kegs into the Blossom Restaurant and Lounge in New York. c. 1950

Canadian Laundry Driver
On the job. 1954

Wagon Train
Dave Cass, an actor in the series 'Wagon Train' was a Teamster too. He was a member of Local 598. 1965

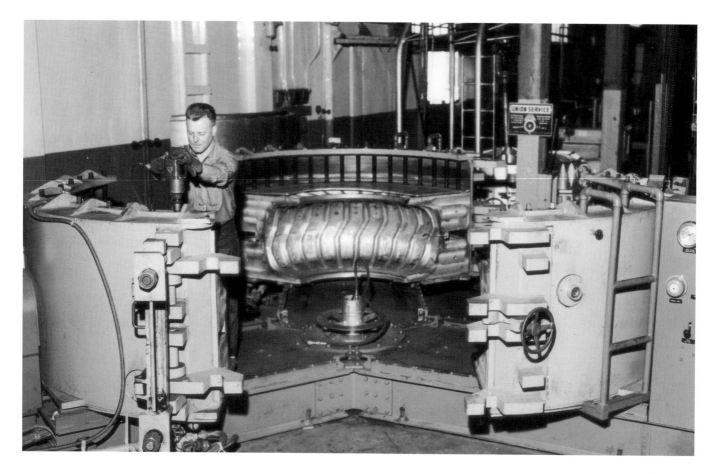

Thompson Aircraft Plant
The San Francisco plant was said to be the only place in the world that recapped airplane tires. A Teamster from Local 665 does the job. 1953

National Trucking Rodeos
These were eagerly anticipated events for members. The 1966 national winners were all Teamsters.

Left:
Teamster Pride
A retired Teamster from Local 35 shows his pride. c. 1965

Below, left:
Breath of Fresh Air
A Teamster loads oxygen tanks to be transported to a local hospital. c. 1956

Below, center:
Trucking Along
Mrs. Ted Owens of Local 291 behind the wheel of her 15-ton dump truck. 1965

Below:
On a Roll
Moving newspaper rolls as the daily printing process begins. 1962

Teamster Ingenuity
*Teamster Ben Evans
points to the see-around
mirror he developed.
1965*

Below:
Lone Star Teamster
*A Dallas Teamster from
Local 745 at work for
Gilbert Systems Co.
c. 1970s*

Below, center:
Tuning Up
*Mechanic working on a
rig engine. c. 1972*

Below, right:
Taking Stock
*Ruth McDonough from
Local 25 working with
stock items. c. 1980s*

Fulfilling a Dream
Teamsters support members' ambitions. Ferris Cassius, a 14-year Teamster veteran, realizes his dream of owning his own business with the help and support of his union brothers. Herb Bailey and Rudy Cook of Local 775 in Denver celebrate the grand opening with Cassius. 1966

A Dangerous Job
Teamsters working with hazardous materials in the 1980s.

The Next 100 Years:

Visions of the Future

The world in 1903 looked very different than it does now. Many of the rights and protections that workers take for granted today were just a dream at the turn of the last century. Standards governing hours of work barely existed. Workplace safety regulations were weak where they existed at all. Child labor laws were nonexistent.

Yet despite the unprecedented pace of change that characterized the 20th Century, Teamsters of today have the same aspirations as Teamsters of old: A fair day's pay for a fair day's work; job security; a safe workplace; good healthcare; a secure retirement; and time to spend with family and friends.

With the challenges to workers' aspirations as formidable as ever, the Teamsters Union has embarked on a wide range of innovative policies and programs aimed at securing another century of growth and prosperity for working men and women.

Changing to Grow
The Teamsters Union has committed massive resources to new organizing initiatives in order to grow the union. 2003

Changing to Grow

By committing massive resources to new, innovative organizing initiatives, the Teamsters Union is leading the North American labor movement in its drive to organize the unorganized.

During an historic Special Convention in 2002, delegates nearly unanimously approved a revamped dues structure that earmarked millions of dollars every year to an Organizing Fund. And in 2003, the union's first-ever conference devoted solely to recruiting new members ratified the program of its newly reconstituted Organizing Department to strategically

Flying High
Local 85 Teamsters celebrate an organizing victory during the San Francisco airport campaign. 2001

organize in Teamsters core industries, target member-rich industries and increase the union's organizing capacity.

The union's emphasis on strategic organizing campaigns has begun to bear fruit. Its impact is felt in such diverse yet traditional Teamsters strongholds as United Parcel Service, where partnerships with local unions are bringing in part-time workers; in the waste industry, by targeting nationwide giants Waste Management and BFI; at beverage companies, taking aim at Coca-Cola and Pepsi merchandisers; in food distribution warehouses; and in freight, carhaul and tankhaul.

Political Strength

Today's Teamsters Union has regained its reputation as the most influential and politically powerful labor organization in the United States.

In recent years, the Teamsters political program and DRIVE—the union's political action committee—have scored

Energized and Organized
*Washington, DC
Teamsters from Local 639
back efforts to recruit new
members. 2003*

major victories in the union's efforts to elect a bipartisan
Teamster majority. The Teamsters political program is based
on members' interests, closely following legislative and regula-
tory issues that impact Teamsters and their families.

In Washington, Ottawa, and state and provincial capitals
throughout North America, Teamsters lobbyists ensure that
the rank-and-file voice is heard loud and clear. Current legislative priorities include union self-governance; extended
unemployment and health care benefits for displaced workers; opposition to trade agreements where labor and environ-
mental standards are not included or enforced; highway safety
improvements; safe transportation of hazardous materials;

Teamster Majority
*The Teamsters Union has
scored major victories in
its effort to elect a
bipartisan Teamster
majority in Congress.*

Fair Trade
5,000 Teamsters march on the U.S. Capitol demanding a fair trade program with China. 2000

immigrant worker rights; prescription drug coverage; worker health and safety; improvement of labor standards; strengthened worker rights and protections; a Patients' Bill of Rights; and strengthened Social Security and Medicare.

A House in Order

In 2002, democratically elected Special Convention delegates approved a new funding structure that will provide financial stability to the union for decades to come. Their work built upon a report by the Blue Ribbon Commission on Union Finances, which was appointed by the General Executive Board to review the Teamsters general treasury and Strike Fund, and to explore ideas and options to best solve the union's fiscal challenges.

No Unsafe Trucks
California Teamsters march to protect U.S. highways from unsafe Mexican trucks. 2001

The Commission, which included 90 International, Joint Council and local union officers and rank-and-file members from every region, called for reforms to generate needed income to create a dedicated Strike Fund with meaningful benefits; fund a new campaign to organize the unorganized;

rebuild Teamster programs and services; and restore the union's financial strength.

Yet despite its formidable ambitions, the dues reform was formulated so as to keep the per capita lower than any other international union; preserve local autonomy and provide new money for locals; be indexed to members' wages; and address the special situation of public employees who in some cases cannot strike.

Financial Strength
General Secretary-Treasurer C. Thomas Keegel led efforts to restructure the union's finances to prepare for the future. 2002

Strong Representation

The real test of a union's worth is found in the value of the contracts it negotiates. The Teamsters is legendary for its ability to win strong contracts, and it continues to win the best agreements in the labor movement regardless of prevailing economic conditions.

Despite a stagnant economy, union negotiators in recent years have won major national master agreements in core industries, including carhaul, where contract victories in 1999 and 2003 preserved health care, boosted pensions and achieved wage gains and job security provisions; freight, where a $1.7 billion National Master Freight Agreement in 2003 provided the best monetary package ever for more than 65,000 members, improving on the previous agreement by some $700 million; and United Parcel Service, where the $10 billion 2002 national master agreement secured the best wage and benefit package in company history, and provided more than 200,000 Teamsters with the industry's strongest job protections.

Under the union's revamped dues structure, a dedicated

Freight Unity
Freight Teamsters ratified the 2003 NMFA with a record 86% of the membership voting yes.

Strike and Defense Fund provides members forced to strike with out-of-work benefits of 10 times the hourly rate. The fund has been an important lever for extracting gains at the bargaining table.

Running a Clean Union

Even before taking office, current General President James P. Hoffa pledged to maintain a union culture that is intolerant of organized crime, and to establish and enforce legitimate, reasonable standards of conduct to safeguard the union and its members against corruption.

To implement the plan, the General Executive Board formed Project RISE (Respect, Integrity, Strength, Ethics) to establish a clear, concise and practical program for members and officers based upon fundamental trade union values and applicable legal requirements. One goal of RISE is to educate officers and members about these values and requirements

UPS Solidarity
UPS workers from California (above) to New York (below) rallied to achieve a strong, $10 billion contract. 2002

and to identify any remaining organized crime influences within the union.

In RISE's exhaustive 526-page report, "The Teamsters: Perception and Reality: An Investigative Study of Organized Crime Influence in the Union," a team of advisors that included FBI investigators, government officials, professors and prosecutors determined that the days of domination and significant infiltration of the Teamsters Union by organized crime were over.

Although the Teamsters have come a long way in rooting out corruption, union leaders realize it is important to operate internal systems that will sustain a commitment to protecting the members and the union.

One-Member, One-Vote
The Hoffa Administration led efforts to codify "one-member, one-vote" into the Teamsters Constitution.
2001

One-Member, One-Vote

Perhaps the most important step in protecting the members' voice in the union occurred at the 2001 International Convention. The Teamsters initiated a new era of union democracy by passing a Hoffa administration resolution to enshrine the principle of one-Teamster, one-vote, as a permanent component of the union's constitution.

This unique direct election of International officers in North America's largest union provided for a secret ballot vote by mail on candidates nominated in open convention by member-elected delegates. At the same time, this landmark action firmly established beyond reasonable doubt that the members are both capable and determined to govern themselves in accordance with the highest principles of democratic trade unionism, whereby the union's power resides entirely with the rank-and-file.

A House United

By setting it's sites on rebuilding the union, the Teamsters have undertaken major changes that have reinvigorated the union and brought its members together as a tight-knit family extending across North America.

Once divided by corrosive internal politics that threatened to tear the union apart, today's Teamsters Union is a house united, focused on pursuing a better future for North America's working families. And as the global economy delivers ever-greater power to an increasingly concentrated group of multinational corporations, today's Teamsters are reaching out to brothers and sisters in every nation to build solidarity and counter common adversaries.

Members Speak
Rank-and-file members participated in the 2001 Convention in greater numbers than ever before.

Planning For Growth
1,400 local union officers committed to a new program to expand membership at the "Changing To Grow" conference. 2003

United
The 2001 Convention was a testament to Teamster solidarity.

Recent changes and changes yet to come harken back to the early beginnings of the union and to its vision of unity, pride and strength. Yet while members continue to struggle for workplace justice as they did 100 years ago, their odds of achieving success are much greater now. Standing on a legacy of high ideals and great sacrifice, today's Teamster looks forward to a future full of promise—the promise of attaining and wielding the means to demand justice and dignity for North America's working men and women.

Smooth Flying
Mechanics and related personnel at Frontier Airlines choose the Teamsters. 2002

Jackpot
Casino parking attendants select Teamsters representation in Detroit. 2000

Public Servants
Canadian Teamsters stand on the front lines in the fight for public safety. 2000

No Right-To-Work
Above left: Colorado Teamsters let legislators know how they feel about anti-worker laws. The Teamsters won in their effort to keep right-to-work legislation from passing in the state. 2001

No To WTO
More than 3,000 Teamsters converged on Seattle to demonstrate against the World Trade Organization. 1999

Political Power

Above: President Bill Clinton honors General President Hoffa at a dinner in New York. 1999

Right: Vice President Al Gore receives the Teamsters endorsement during his presidential bid. 2000

Political Strength
Left: President George W. Bush meets with General President Hoffa at Teamsters headquarters. 2002

Below: Minority Leader Richard Gephardt (D-MO), the son of a Teamster, addresses the Teamsters Political and Legislative Coordinators Conference. 2002

Unity Pays
Warehouse workers from Missouri, Kansas and Oklahoma celebrate their victory at Associated Wholesale Grocers. 2000

Back to Basic
*Local 890 Teamsters
celebrate their victory at
Basic Vegetable Products,
ending a two-year strike.
2001*

Delivering Victory
*Below: Carhaul Teamsters
celebrate the 2003
contract that protected
health care and enhanced
job security.*

Unions Unite
*General President Hoffa
and UNITE President
Bruce Raynor kick off a
joint organizing
campaign.
2003*

100-Year Locals

Congratulations to the 18 Teamster Locals
also celebrating their
100th Anniversary in 2003.

Local 20 Toledo, Ohio	**Local 179** Joliet, Illinois
Local 25 Boston, Massachusetts	**Local 221** Minneapolis, Minnesota
Local 42 Lynn, Massachusetts	**Local 229** Scranton, Pennsylvania
Local 50 Belleville, Illinois	**Local 294** Albany, New York
Local 70 Oakland, California	**Local 313** Tacoma, Washington
Local 85 San Francisco, California	**Local 641** Union, New Jersey
Local 90 Des Moines, Iowa	**Local 705** Chicago, Illinois
Local 120 St. Paul, Minnesota	**Local 710** Chicago, Illinois
Local 162 Portland, Oregon	**Local 734** Chicago, Illinois

General Presidents

Cornelius P. Shea
Boston, Massachusetts
1903-1907

Daniel J. Tobin
Boston, Massachusetts
1907-1952

Dave Beck
Seattle, Washington
1952-1957

James R. Hoffa
Detroit, Michigan
1957-1971

Frank E. Fitzsimmons
Detroit, Michigan
1971-1981

Roy Williams
Kansas City, Missouri
1981-1983

Jackie Presser
Cleveland, Ohio
1983-1988

William J. McCarthy
Boston, Massachusetts
1988-1992

Ron Carey
New York, New York
1992-1997

James P. Hoffa
Detroit, Michigan
1999-Present

General Secretary-Treasurers

Edward L. Turley
Chicago, Illinois
1903-1905

Thomas L. Hughes
Chicago, Illinois
1905-1941

John M. Gillespie
Boston, Massachusetts
1941-1946

John F. English
Boston, Massachusetts
1946-1969

Thomas F. Flynn
South Bend, Indiana
1969-1972

Murray W. Miller
Dallas, Texas
1972-1976

Ray Schoessling
Chicago, Illinois
1976-1984

Weldon L. Mathis
Atlanta, Georgia
1985-1991

Thomas L. Sever
Jeannette, Pennsylvania
1992-1999

C. Thomas Keegel
Minneapolis, Minnesota
1999-Present

Acknowledgments

100TH ANNIVERSARY PROJECT

Bret Caldwell
Director of
Communicatio

Sally Payne
Associate Direct
Communicatio

Karin Jones
Project Coordina

Per Bernstein
Editor

Jeff Jones
Designer

David White
Production

CONTRIBUTING ST

David Kamera

Joel Coffidis

Jim Carlile

Amy Quarles

SUPPORT STAFF

Anna Kerney

Heather Collins

Yvette Robinson

Dale Woytko

Don Barton

Rachel Moeller

e would also like to give special thanks to the llowing individuals for king the time to share heir knowledge and erience of the union's history with us. This ject would have been impossible without their help.

Cheryl Johnson

Leo Deaner

Steve Sullivan

Gary Witlen

Rich Leebove

Norma Bartus

Carolyn Moore

Don Dunaway

Cindy Impala

Brian Rainville

Jim Saah